THE STRATEGY OF PUTS AND CALLS

THE STRATEGY OF PUTS AND CALLS

SELLING STOCK OPTIONS
FOR MAXIMUM PROFIT
WITH MINIMUM RISK

ZAVEN A. DADEKIAN

CORINTHIAN EDITIONS   NEW YORK 1968

TO
MY WIFE
Arline

Preface

I have long felt the need for a book that dealt comprehensively with the complexities of buying and especially selling stock options. It is a fast growing segment of the investment field, as we in the securities industry know from the growth of the flourishing option business. But would-be option sellers without experience have had no single source book to which they could turn for all the information they needed about option transactions.

This book fills that need. An extremely successful young option writer has, for the first time, set down on paper a logical and quantitative approach to a complex branch of the investment business in which hunches based on experience have often been the guiding principles. The book considers all the factors of successful option selling. Examples are freely used to illustrate the principles discussed. I think that this book will be of interest to all investors.

Richard Neuberger
Manager, Option Department
Scheinman, Hochstin & Trotta, Inc.

Acknowledgements

The author wishes to express his thanks to Richard Neuberger, Michael Epstein and Harry Schacter, whose encouragement was invaluable. Thanks are also due to David Wilbourn who offered valuable suggestions and criticisms of the manuscript, and to Joseph Lefrak and William Harnett who reviewed the chapters on taxes and margin respectively. The difficult job of typing the manuscript was undertaken by my wife, who added clerical duties to her role as mother of three children.

Contents

THE STRATEGY OF
PUTS AND CALLS

I

Introduction

Most active investors in today's stock markets are aware of the existence of option transactions involving Puts, Calls, and their combinations. The financial pages of the *Wall Street Journal* and other financial newspapers daily advertise opportunities to purchase and sell stock options. Indeed, it has been reported by the financial press that option transactions are one of the fastest growing branches of the securities business.

A Put contract is an option, for which a premium is paid, to *sell* a specified amount of stock at a fixed price during a stated time period. A Call contract is an option, for which a premium is paid, to *buy* a specified amount of stock at a fixed price during a stated time period. Straddles, Strips, Straps, and Spreads are the commonly accepted names for combinations of these two basic contracts.

All option transactions involve both a buyer and a seller.

Introduction

This book discusses both buying and selling options, although it is directed primarily to the option seller or "option writer." The mechanics of selling stock options are not well known by the general public and even by much of the investment community.

Most options are bought for purely speculative purposes by both sophisticated investors and relative novices. Sometimes these transactions are spectacularly successful. More often they are not. Without considering the merits of speculative option purchases, it is important to recognize that their attractiveness as a speculative vehicle is appreciated by a large and growing number of investors.

Options are also purchased by sophisticated investors as insurance or protection for some other investment. This use of option purchases as part of a conservative investment program is less well-known to investors than the speculative uses, but it is growing in popularity. Thus the option writer has a broad spectrum of potential customers buying options for both speculative and conservative investment programs.

The number of option buyers, although growing fast, is still probably less than 1% of the total number of investors in common stocks. Option writers are an even more exclusive fraternity. They include institutions holding a portfolio of common stocks, such as insurance companies, mutual funds, pension funds, university endowment funds, etc. These institutions usually sell options as an adjunct rather than as the prime purpose of their investment programs. There are individuals, however, who engage in option writing as an important, if not dominant, feature of their otherwise conventional investment programs. They include a surprisingly large number of sophisticated European investors who both purchase and sell options on American stocks extensively.

14

This book is directed to investors attracted by the substantial potential rewards of an active option-writing program whether it is a dominant or a supplemental feature of their investment program. Successful option writing requires a degree of market sophistication and experience well above that possessed by the average investor. The complicated margin rules, tax regulations, record keeping, negotiating skill and time available, inevitably limit those who can or wish to write options. Psychological factors, such as the ability to make and stick with almost instantaneous decisions involving substantial sums of money, also limit the number of people writing options. Availability of capital is another obvious limitation. Because option writers deal in round-lots, there is undoubtedly a minimum amount of capital necessary to sustain an active program.

The preceding is not to imply that all option writers must be highly trained finance men. An intelligent investor able to make quick, sound decisions and willing to study this book can learn at least the basic rules of the game. A proper option-writing program is an essentially conservative, though sophisticated approach to investment. However, there are degrees of conservatism. The inexperienced option writer can be cautious initially and change to a program involving more risk as he gains in experience and profits.

The incentive for option writing is the possibility of a return of 15% to 40% on invested capital. The percentage depends on the degree of risk an option writer is willing to assume and the skill with which the program is executed. As in any investment program involving risk, luck is a factor. It is a feature of option writing, however, that luck is a much less important factor in consistently realizing comparable profits than in conventional investment programs. A satisfactory return on investment can and should

Introduction

be achieved whether the market goes up or down or stays stationary year after year. As in any stock investment program, there is a premium on accurate estimates of the general course of the market and the movement of specific stocks. The very nature of option writing, however, allows for substantially greater margins of error in achieving success than in conventional investment programs.

The option buyer can make a several hundred percent return on his investment in an individual transaction. The option writer cannot realize such a return on an individual transaction. However, a well-executed option-writing program will produce profits on invested capital which are outstanding by any standards. Some investors thrive on the excitement of daily fluctuations of their stocks, exhilarated by price advances and dismayed by declines. The option writer will not find this excitement, because he is much less affected by daily price fluctuations. At the time he writes his option, his freedom of action is curtailed for the specified time period, and his maximum profit is predetermined by the premium he receives.

Successful option writing requires substantial time, money, and knowledge. However, the rewards relative to the risks are also substantial. Indeed, the author believes that for a comparable expected annual return on investment there is a much lower level of risk in option writing than in a conventional investment program. This is the payoff for the study, experience, and the continuous time and attention that must be devoted to an option-writing program.

The expertise required for developing an option-writing program has never been easy to obtain. The author knows of no one place where the margin rules, techniques for evaluating premiums, and the pertinent tax laws are all available. Except for a few highly specialized stockbrokers specializing in option sales, there has been no way to learn even the basic rules. Even with the best intentions, these "option brokers" have a limited amount of time available to educate clients. Trial and error, sometimes costly, has been the option writer's school. This book is intended to offer an alternative. While the author hopes that existing option writers will find the information here helpful, it is not just to them that this book is directed; it is primarily written so that intelligent investors may evaluate the suitability of doing their own option writing, and develop the necessary background to proceed with such a program if they so wish. To compensate for a lack of experience, the author has devised two sets of graphs (see pages 74–79 and 98–103) to help quickly evaluate the potential annual return on investment of a given option and the attractiveness of that option bid in relation to similar previous bids.

The investment community usually pictures the successful option writer as a very experienced, if not professional investor with a large portfolio of stocks worth perhaps several hundred thousand dollars. His option-writing program is essentially conservative, and is an adjunct to his conventional investment program. Perhaps he makes an annual 15% to 20% return on his investment in option writing. This is a true picture of many successful option writers. However, it is possible to realize a considerably higher return on investment in option writing. It is this potential return which attracts some would-be option writers who understand option-writing techniques only superficially and who have no overall strategy for success. While these option writers may do well for a time, their lack of background and their inability to evaluate the risks in writing options inevitably lead to disappointment and failure. These would-be option writers tend to be investors with little experience and little capital.

The author believes that extensive investment experience and a capital of hundreds of thousands of dollars are not necessary to a successful option writer. His own experience is a case in point. The author is a scientist-businessman with no elaborate training in investments. He began his option-writing program about five years ago with a capital of about $10,000. Since then, spending about ten hours a month on his program, he has consistently realized a compounded 30% to 40% annual return on invested capital, multiplying the original investment many times. To realize these returns, he deliberately embarked on a high-risk option-writing program. Success resulted only because he developed an overall strategy based on the principles outlined in this book.

In a successful high-risk program, an option writer can double his capital every three or four years whether or not the stock market rises. A $10,000 initial investment can become $100,000 in ten years or $250,000 in fifteen years.

The author envisions a new breed of option writers. They are young business or professional men with disciplined minds, who are interested in the stock market, comfortable with figures, and used to making substantive decisions objectively. They will be anxious to accept the challenge of mastering the admittedly complex strategy of successful option writing. Their reward will be the possibility of financial independence after a few years of option writing. Their initial capital investment is well within the reach of most business and professional people.

There are other incentives too. In today's business and professional world, individual achievement is diluted by the performance of colleagues in the organization. Option writing is a one man show. The degree of success depends only on the capacity of the individual, and the satisfaction of success is all his. Option writers invariably enjoy their hobby, which can be carried on without interrupting a career. In fact, the experience gained in option writing can enhance success in business or the professions.

II

Stock Options Defined

A stock option is a legal contract between buyer and seller under which the seller, for a premium, guarantees the buyer his right to exercise a privilege under strictly defined terms. The type of privilege determines the type of stock option.

The Call option grants the buyer the privilege of buying or "calling from" the seller 100 shares of stock under terms of the contract.

The Put option grants the buyer the privilege of selling or "putting to" the seller 100 shares of stock under terms of the contract.

The Call and the Put are the two basic stock options from which all others are derived. A Put and a Call contract are reproduced at the end of this chapter.

The following elements are specified in all option contracts:

1. The name of the stock and number of shares involved. Units of 100 shares are traded exclusively in normal transactions.

2. The time for which the contract is in force. Options are commonly, but not exclusively, written for 30 days, 65 days, 95 days, six months and 10 days, and one year.

3. The contract price at which the privilege can be exercised. This price is commonly referred to as the "striking price" or "strike price." The author prefers the latter term and uses it throughout the book. The strike price is usually the market price or close to the market price of the stock at the time the option sale is executed. The strike price will be reduced during the life of the contract by the amount of cash dividends, stock splits, rights, etc. that may be declared.

4. The proper execution of the option contract is guaranteed when a member firm of the New York Stock Exchange endorses it at the time of sale. On or before the expiration date, no later than 3:15 P.M., the contract must be physically presented to the endorsing firm for the privilege to be exercised. The owner of the option and his broker are responsible for meeting the terms of execution.

5. When the option contract is agreed to, the buyer pays a cash premium. The seller receives the premium less a differential paid to a third party for arranging the transaction. The premium is deposited into the seller's brokerage account as cash. The amount of the premium is a major consideration for both buyer and seller. Premiums for options are negotiated for each transaction. The negotiating skill of the buyer and seller and their respective brokers, the stock involved, the duration of the contract, the strike price, and the type of option are all factors which determine the premium.

The buyer has the option of exercising or not exercising his privilege to buy or sell the stock at any time up to the expiration of the option contract. The option writer has no such choice. He must live up to the terms of the contract if and when the buyer chooses to exercise his privilege. In the language of option transactions, exercising a privilege is often referred to as "exercising an option."

Straddle options are a combination of two separate option contracts, a Call and a Put, executed simultaneously, for the same time period, at the same strike price. Both the Call and the Put may be exercised independently during the life of the contract.

Strip options are a combination of three separate options, two Puts and a Call, executed simultaneously, for the same time period, at the same strike price. Strips can be considered a combination of a Straddle and a Put. Each of the three options may be exercised independently during the life of the contract.

Strap options are a combination of three separate options, two Calls and a Put, executed simultaneously, for the same time period, at the same strike price. Straps can also be considered a combination of a Straddle and a Call. Each of the three options can be exercised independently during the life of the contract.

Spread options are a combination of a Put and a Call, executed simultaneously, but for different time periods or for different strike prices, or both. Usually the strike price for the Call is higher than that for the Put. The difference between the prices is called a "spread."

Stock Options Defined

WILKINS - ROSE INC.
Members Put and Call Brokers and Dealers Association, Inc.
PUT AND CALL OPTIONS

GUARANTEED BY MEMBERS N. Y. STOCK EXCHANGE
111 BROADWAY, N. Y. 10006   WORTH 4-2274

Copyr. 1957, Put and Call Brokers and Dealers Assn., Inc.

New York, N. Y. _____

MAY 2 9 1968

Kur Halur Rrreiurд, the BEARER may DELIVER to the endorser ONE HUNDRED (100) shares of the _____ **common**

stock of the _____ McLean Trucking Co. (MLN) _____

at _____ Thirty two and six seven five _____ Dollars ($32.675 _____) per share

ANY TIME WITHIN _____ Twenty one _____ days from date.

THIS STOCK OPTION CONTRACT MUST BE PRESENTED, AS SPECIFIED BELOW, TO THE ENDORSING FIRM BEFORE THE EXPIRATION OF THE EXACT TIME LIMIT. IT CANNOT BE EXERCISED BY TELEPHONE.

DURING THE LIFE OF THIS OPTION:

1. (a) — the contract price hereof shall be reduced by the value of any cash dividend on the day the stock goes ex-dividend;
(b) — where the Option is entitled to rights and/or warrants the contract price shall be reduced by the value of same as fixed by the opening sale thereof on the day the stock sells ex-rights and/or ex-warrants.

2. (a) — in the event of stock splits, reverse splits or other similar action by the above-mentioned corporation, this Option shall become an Option for the equivalent in new securities when duly listed for trading and the total contract price shall not be reduced;
(b) — stock dividends or the equivalent due-bills shall be attached to the stock covered hereby, when and if this Option is exercised, and the total contract price shall not be reduced.

Upon presentation to the endorser of this Option attached to a comparison ticket in the manner and time specified, the endorser agrees to accept notice of the Bearer's exercise by stamping the comparison, and this acknowledgment shall constitute a contract and shall be controlling with respect to delivery of the stock and settlement in accordance with New York Stock Exchange usage.

EXPIRES _____ June 19 19 68

3:15 P. M., NEW YORK, N. Y. TIME

I Nọ 185

SOLD BY MEMBER
PUT & CALL
BROKERS & DEALERS
ASSOCIATION, INC.

The undersigned acts as intermediary only, without obligation other than to obtain a New York Stock Exchange firm as Endorser.

Wilkins - Rose Inc.

24   **PUT OPTION**

THIS CONTRACT BOUGHT THRU

GODNICK & SON, INC.

Members Put and Call Brokers and Dealers Association, Inc.

PUT AND CALL OPTIONS

GUARANTEED BY MEMBERS N. Y. STOCK EXCHANGE

30 BROAD STREET, N. Y. 4   HANOVER 2-3822

New York, N. Y. February 1st., 19 68

For Value Received, the BEARER may CALL on the endorser for ONE HUNDRED (100) shares of the

stock of the Astrodata Inc. (ADA) common

at eleven and seven eighths Dollars ($ 11.875) per share

ANY TIME WITHIN six months and seven eleven days from date.

THIS STOCK OPTION CONTRACT MUST BE PRESENTED AS SPECIFIED BELOW, TO THE ENDORSING FIRM BEFORE THE EXPIRATION OF THE EXACT TIME LIMIT. IT CANNOT BE EXERCISED BY TELEPHONE.

DURING THE LIFE OF THIS OPTION:

1. (a) — the contract price hereof shall be reduced by the value of any cash dividend on the day the stock goes ex-dividend;

(b) — where the Option is entitled to rights and/or warrants the contract price shall be reduced by the value of same as fixed by the opening sale thereof on the day the stock sells ex-rights and/or warrants.

2. (a) — in the event of stock splits, reverse splits or other similar action by the above-mentioned corporation, this Option shall become an Option for the equivalent in new securities when duly listed for trading and the total contract price shall not be reduced;

(b) — stock dividends or the equivalent due-bills shall be attached to the stock covered hereby, when and if this Option is exercised, and the total contract price shall not be reduced.

Upon presentation to the endorser of this Option attached to a comparison ticket in the manner and time specified, the endorser agrees to accept notice of the Bearer's exercise by stamping the comparison, and this acknowledgment shall constitute a contract and shall be controlling with respect to delivery of the stock and settlement in accordance with New York Stock Exchange usage.

EXPIRES August 12th 19 68

3:15 P. M., NEW YORK, N. Y. TIME

Q No 347

SOLD BY MEMBER

PUT & CALL
BROKERS & DEALERS
ASSOCIATION, I

The undersigned acts as intermediary only, without obligation other than to obtain a New York Stock Exchange firm as Endorser.

CALL OPTION   25

III

Speculative Uses for Stock Options

The buyer of a Call option for speculation has paid a premium for the privilege of buying 100 shares of stock at a fixed price during a specified time period. He hopes and expects that that stock price will go up. If the option expires and he has not exercised it because the market price of the stock is below the strike price, he will have forfeited the premium. In this case it would not be advantageous to exercise the option because the stock can be purchased in the market at a lower price. If the strike price and market price are identical, he may or may not exercise his option. If he does, he has not received any benefit from the option since the stock is available for purchase in the market at the same price. If the market price is above the strike price, it will be advantageous for him to exercise his option. The stock can then be immediately resold at the market price at a profit, or held in the stock account for further possible appreciation. The buyer of a Call will make a profit on the overall transaction when exercising his option only if the market price of the stock is sufficiently above the strike price to offset the cost of the premium.

The timing for exercising a Call to maximum advantage can be difficult. The option buyer may exercise it before expiration thinking that the price may be at its peak. If he waits until expiration, however, the price might advance further. On the other hand, the price could decline, reducing or eliminating his profit. Tax considerations further complicate the option buyer's timing. He can realize a long-term gain only by holding his Call more than six months. This puts a premium on holding six month and 10 day Calls until expiration, although the option buyer may be sorely tempted to exercise his Call for a sure but short-term profit.

Stock options are contracts having property value and may be sold for their value. In practice, profitable stock options held over six months are sold before expiration to the option buyer's broker. Since the option contract represents a capital asset held longer than six months, it qualifies as a long-term gain for tax purposes. In this case, it is the broker who actually exercises the option, realizes the profit, deducts brokerage expenses and remits the net to the option buyer as the sale price of his option. Examples of this procedure are included below.

Let us say that a buyer has purchased a Call option for six months and 10 days on ABC Company for a premium of $400. The strike price was $20 which happened to be the market price when the contract was agreed to. The buyer has held the option to expiration because he did not feel it was advantageous to exercise it before that time. When and if he exercises his option to purchase 100 shares at the strike price, the buyer must pay brokerage fees as though he had purchased the stock on the market. For purposes of illustration, these brokerage fees are not included, although in computing profits and losses on all option transactions, the brokerage fees are a significant factor. Also omitted in the illustrations are any rights, dividends, etc. that may have reduced the strike price slightly.

	MARKET PRICE AT EXPIRATION	STRIKE PRICE	PREMIUM	PROFIT (LOSS)
Case I	10	20	400	(400)
Case II	20	20	400	(400)
Case III	22	20	400	(200)
Case IV	24	20	400	0
Case V	30	20	400	600

CASE I—The market price is below the strike price, and the option will not be exercised at the strike price of $20 since the stock can be purchased in the market at $10. The $400 paid for the premium is lost.

CASE II—The market price and the stock price are identical. If the option buyer wishes to purchase the stock and hold it in his account for possible future appreciation, he may exercise his option or purchase the stock in the market. He may also elect to let the option expire without exercising it. In any event, his option has not proved advantageous to him, and the $400 he paid for it is a loss.

CASE III—The market price is higher than the strike price, and it is advantageous to exercise the option. The buyer pays $2,000 to purchase 100 shares of the stock under terms of the Call option. The premium was $400. The total outlay then is $2,400 for stock having a market value of $2,200. The overall loss on the transaction is $200.

CASE IV—The market price is higher than the strike price, and the option will be exercised. The $2,000 paid for 100 shares of the stock under terms of the Call option plus the $400 premium for the Call exactly equals the $2,400 market price for the stock. The buyer has broken even.

CASE V—The market price is considerably higher than the strike price, and the option is exercised. The cost of the 100 shares of stock is $2,000, and the market value of stock is $3,000. The stock can be immediately resold for a gross profit of $1,000 and a net profit of $600, after deducting the $400 premium. It can also be held for future appreciation.

Since the option itself is a contract having property value, it can itself be sold for its $1,000 value just before expiration, but more than six months after the Call was purchased. The option buyer's broker purchases the Call for $1,000 exercising the option by purchasing stock at $20 and selling at $30. The Call itself is thus sold for $1,000, and the net profit after deducting the $400 paid for the premium is $600. The $600 qualifies for a long-term capital gain. Had the option buyer himself exercised his option by purchasing at $20 and immediately reselling the stock to realize his $1,000 gross profit, the $600 net profit after deduction of the premium, would have been a short-term gain.

The purchase of a Call in anticipation of a stock price increase is generally considered speculative relative to the purchase of 100 shares of the stock in the market. Even if the buyer is correct in anticipating an upward movement in the stock price, this movement must be substantial and must take place during the life of his Call to result in profit. In the examples above, an increase of about 20% is necessary before profits accrue. By contrast, the purchaser of 100 shares of the stock in the market has already made $400 when the buyer of the Call has only broken even. Moreover, the outright purchaser of the stock can hold on to it indefinitely and can wait to sell at a profit if his estimated time for price appreciation is incorrect.

Case V above illustrates a situation most attractive to the purchaser of Calls. If instead of investing $2,000 in 100 shares of ABC stock, the same $2,000 were used to pay the premiums on five Calls, the leverage for profits increases dramatically. With the stock going from $20 to $30, the holder of 100 shares would show a profit of $1,000, but the purchaser of five Calls (i.e. options to buy 500 shares) would make $3,000.

Case I illustrates a situation where—in retrospect—the purchase of a Call can be considered conservative rather than speculative compared to the outright purchase of 100 shares. With a decline in price to $10, the purchaser of ABC stock at $20 has a $1,000 paper loss. He may take this loss by selling, or he may wait for the stock price to advance. The purchaser of a Call has merely lost his premium of $400. If he finds the stock attractive at $10, he can purchase it in the market and be in the same situation as the original purchaser of 100 shares at $20.

The buyer of a Put option for speculation hopes and expects that the price of the stock will go down. He has paid a premium to the option writer for the privilege of selling him 100 shares of stock at a fixed price any time during the life of the contract. The option writer must purchase the stock at the strike price less dividends, rights, etc., whenever it is "put" to him during the life of the option. The buyer of the Put will find it advantageous to sell the 100 shares to the option writer only if the market price of the stock is below the strike price. He can then sell the stock if it is already in his account, or buy it in the market and then sell it to the option writer at the higher strike price. If the option expires unexercised, because the market price is above the strike price, the premium will be forfeited. If the Put buyer owns 100 shares of ABC stock, having purchased them either before or after the option was purchased and if the market price is higher than the strike price, he will not exercise his option to sell to the Put seller, since he can get more for the stock in the market. Assuming the market price and strike price are identical, the Put buyer may or may not exercise his option to sell to the option writer if he already owns the stock. There is no advantage to his doing so, however, since he can get the same price in the market. If he does not already own the stock, he will definitely not find it advantageous to exercise his option. To do so he would have to buy the stock at the market price, and by deducting brokerage fees, take a net loss.

The problem of timing the exercise of a Put option is the same as for the exercise of a Call. Premature exercise of the Put may limit possible profits if the price of the stock continues to decline. An option can only be exercised once. Tax considerations also influence the timing for exercising a Put. A profitable Put, held for more than six months and then sold for its value to a broker, is the only way to enjoy a long-term capital gain on a stock whose market price has declined.

For purposes of illustration let us say that a buyer has purchased a six month and 10 day Put option on ABC Co. for a premium of $300 at the strike price of $20 which happened to be the market price when the Put was purchased. The premium for a Put is usually less than that for a Call at the same strike price and for the same time period, since there is much less of a demand for Puts. Assume that the option has been held to expiration. Brokerage fees for buying and selling stock, and any reduction of the strike price owing to dividends, rights, etc. have been omitted.

	MARKET PRICE AT EXPIRATION	STRIKE PRICE	PREMIUM	PROFIT (LOSS)
Case I	30	20	300	(300)
Case II	20	20	300	(300)
Case III	18	20	300	(100)
Case IV	17	20	300	0
Case V	10	20	300	700

CASE I—The market price is above the strike price and the option will not be exercised at the strike price of $20, since the stock can be sold in the market at $30. The $300 premium is lost.

CASE II—The market price and strike price are identical. The Put buyer will not find it advantageous to purchase stock in the market at expiration and deliver it to the seller of the Put at the same price because he will realize no profit and he will have to pay brokerage expenses. The option will be allowed to expire. If the Put buyer owned 100 shares of ABC stock (bought before or during the life of the Put), he may sell them either in the market, or to the Put seller, or he may hold on to them for possible price appreciation.

CASE III—The market price is lower than the strike price, and it is advantageous to the option buyer to exercise his option. He can buy 100 shares of the stock in the market for $1,800 and sell it for $2,000 to the Put seller for a gross profit of $200. Having paid $300 for the premium, his overall net loss is $100.

CASE IV—The market price is still lower than the strike price, and it is advantageous to exercise the option. The Put buyer can purchase 100 shares of ABC stock in the market for $1,700 and sell to the Put seller for $2,000 for a $300 gross profit. The premium cost $300, so that the option buyer breaks even.

33

Speculative Uses for Stock Options

CASE V—The market price is substantially lower than the strike price, and the option is exercised. The Put seller can purchase 100 shares of ABC stock for $1,000 in the market and sell it to the Put seller for $2,000. The net profit is $700 (gross profit of $1,000 less the $300 premium). The Put option itself, as a contract having property value, could have been sold for its $1,000 value just before expiration, but at least six months and one day after purchase to achieve a long-term capital gain.

Purchase of a Put in anticipation of a stock price decline should be compared to a short sale, the alternate approach to profit in this situation. The short seller could borrow 100 shares of ABC stock from his broker and immediately sell it. In his short account he must deposit not only the entire proceeds from the sale but an additional 80% of the sale price as cash security. There is no time limit on when the short seller must actually buy 100 shares of ABC stock and deliver it to the broker. He will make a profit if and when he can close out his short sale by purchasing the stock in the market at a lower price than that for which he sold the borrowed stock. If the price rises, however, the short seller will have to increase the cash security in his short account according to Stock Exchange rules. Of course, the higher the stock price the less likely that the short position will ever become profitable. The danger of short selling is that there is no theoretical limit to the amount of cash investment which may be necessary to maintain the short position and no limit to the possible loss. The ultimate loss will be the difference between the cost price of the stock when finally purchased to replace the stock borrowed, and the sale price of the borrowed stock when the short position was established.

The purchaser of a Put has definite advantages over the short seller as well as obvious disadvantages. The Put purchaser has the considerable advantage that he can never lose more than the premium paid, and he has a large potential gain for a small, fixed investment. The disadvantages are that the Put purchaser may only realize his profit within the limited life of the contract and that the completed transaction must result in enough profit to compensate for the premium paid.

The buyer of a Straddle option for speculation has purchased both a Put and a Call simultaneously for the same stock. He may exercise either, both, or neither. He hopes that during the duration of the contract, the stock price will fluctuate widely—either up or down—from the strike price. Since he has purchased two options, he has paid approximately twice the premium he would have paid if he had bought either a Put or a Call. On the other hand, because the stock price will probably be either higher or lower than the strike price, he should find it advantageous to exercise one of his options at expiration.

In practice, either the Put or the Call portion of the Straddle is usually exercised. But in some circumstances both options are exercised. For example, suppose the price of the stock advances above the strike price to the point where the Straddle buyer exercises his Call before expiration at a handsome profit. His Put option is still in force. After the exercise of the Call, the stock price plunges below the strike price. The Put can then also be exercised profitably. Occasionally the Straddle options expire with the market price of the stock exactly the same as the strike price. In this unfortunate situation both options are allowed to expire, and the premium for the Straddle will be a total loss.

To illustrate: A buyer has purchased a Straddle option for six months and 10 days on ABC Co. for $700 at the strike price of $20 which happens to be the market price when the Straddle is purchased. Changes in the strike price of the Put and Call options due to declaration of dividends, etc. and the brokerage fees are omitted.

	MARKET PRICE AT EXPIRATION	STRIKE PRICE	PREMIUM	PROFIT (LOSS)
Case I	10	20	700	300
Case II	13	20	700	0
Case III	18	20	700	(500)
Case IV	20	20	700	(700)
Case V	30	20	700	300

CASE I—The market price is well below the strike price, and the Put is exercised. Stock is purchased in the market at $10 and sold to the option writer at $20 for a $1,000 profit on the 100 shares. After deducting the Straddle premium of $700, net profit is $300. The Call is allowed to expire unexercised.

CASE II—The market price is lower than the strike price. The Put is exercised, and the Call is allowed to expire. If stock is bought in the market at $13 and sold at the strike price of $20, the $700 profit would exactly equal the $700 premium paid for the Straddle, and the option buyer has broken even. If the price of the stock had declined to $10 during the life of the Straddle and 100 shares had been purchased in the market, they could have been sold at the strike price for the same profit as in Case I.

CASE III—The market price is below the strike price. The Put is exercised, and the Call is allowed to expire. If stock is purchased in the market at $18 and sold at the strike price of $20, there would be a $200 profit on 100 shares. The Straddle premium was $700, so the net loss is $500. But suppose the market price advanced to $30 during the life of the option before plunging to $18 at expiration. The Straddle buyer could then have exercised his Call (buying at the strike price of $20 from the option writer and selling in the market at $30) for a gross profit of $1,000. At expiration, the Put is exercised and the total net profit from both transactions, after deducting the premium, is $500.

CASE IV—The market price and the strike price are identical, and if the options have not previously been exercised, they are allowed to expire. The market price may never have fluctuated sufficiently from the strike price during the life of the option to make the exercise of either option attractive. If during the life of the option the market price had advanced to $30, the Call could have been exercised for a profit of $1,000 as in Case III. Suppose further that the market price later plunged to $10 and 100 shares of ABC stock was purchased in the market. At expiration, the Put could have been exercised and this stock could have been sold to the Straddle seller or in the market at $20 for a $1,000 profit. The net profit on the two transactions after deducting the premium for the Straddle, is $1,300. This profit was achieved with no net change in the price of the stock within the contract period.

CASE V—The market price is well above the strike price and the Call is exercised, resulting in $300 net profit ($1,000 gross profit less $700 premium). The break-even market price in this case was $27. Had the market price of the stock declined below the strike price during the life of the Straddle, and 100 shares of ABC stock been bought in the market, the Put could have been exercised profitably.

A Spread option is a modification of the Straddle. It also consists of a Put and a Call, but there is a "spread" between the strike prices, the strike price of the Call normally being higher and that of the Put lower than the market price of the stock when the contract is agreed to. The premium is lower than that paid for a Straddle, but so are the possi-

Speculative Uses for Stock Options

bilities of profit. Compared to a Straddle, market price movements in either direction must be larger for comparable profits.

A Strip option is a combination of a Straddle and a Put (i.e. one Call and two Puts). It will be attractive to the buyer who expects a decline in the stock price but who wants to hedge his position in case the stock advances. Because of the Straddle aspect, the buyer may also be interested in the chance of profit through fluctuations in the market price above and below the strike price.

A Strap option is a Straddle and a Call (i.e. two Calls and one Put). The buyer expects the stock to advance, but wishes to hedge with the Put in case it declines.

Both the Strip and the Strap purchasers must count on covering three premiums before realizing a profit.

In practice, option buyers do not often buy Spreads, Strips, and Straps for speculative purposes.

IV

Protective and Trading Uses for Stock Options

Many sophisticated investors buy options to limit a possible loss when making another investment, or to protect a paper profit on a previous investment. Options can also be used for short-term buying and selling with limited risk. Here are examples of such uses:

CASE I—The investor, feeling basically optimistic about a price increase ("bullish") in the stock of ABC Company, buys 100 shares at a market price of $20. But wishing to protect himself against a possible decline, he simultaneously buys a Put option for six months and 10 days, paying a premium of $300, at a strike price of $20. No matter how low the stock falls during the period of the Put contract, he can always sell his shares to the option writer at $20, the strike price, losing only the premium. If the stock price advances, the Put option is his insurance against a subsequent price decline below the strike price. If the stock price goes higher than $23, he makes a net profit after deducting the Put premium.

Under federal income tax laws, the acquisition of a Put is considered equivalent to a short sale with certain rules applying that make it difficult to achieve a long-term capital gain on stock associated with the Put. Purchase of stock and acquisition of a Put on the same day as in the Case above is not regarded as a short sale. The premium paid for the Put is added to the purchase price of the stock as the tax basis for cost of the stock which in the Case above is $23 per share.

CASE II—The investor feels basically pessimistic ("bearish") about ABC Company stock at $20, and sells 100 shares short. To protect himself from a price rise, he purchases a Call for six months and 10 days simultaneously with the short sale at the strike price of $20 and a premium of $400. If the stock price advances rather than declines, the investor's loss is limited to the $400 he paid for the premium. Let us say that the price advances to $30 at the expiration of the Call. Rather than buy the stock in the market at $30 to cover his short sale, he can exercise his Call at $20 and deliver this stock to cover his short sale. Again, only the $400 premium for the Call is lost. Without this insurance he would have lost $1,000 to cover the short sale. If the investor is correct in his assessment, and the stock price declines to $10, he can purchase the stock in the market at that price and deliver it to cover the short sale previously made at $20. His gross profit is $1,000; his net profit then is $600 ($1,000 less the $400 Call premium). In the case of short sales, this type of insurance is cheap indeed.

In Cases I and II above, why did the investor not purchase a Call if he felt "bullish" and a Put if he felt "bearish," rather than buying 100 shares and a Put, and a short sale of 100 shares and a Call respectively? His risk would have been limited to the cost of the premium just as it was in Cases I and II. Moreover, he would not have had to invest cash for the purchase of the stock or security for selling short. The answer is: flexibility in trading. Suppose in Case I the stock advances to $24 and the investor sells his 100 shares for a profit of $400. Then the stock drops back to the strike price or below, and he purchases another 100 shares, enjoying the same security for the duration of his Put. If the stock advances again, he again sells his shares. This process can be repeated several times, each time for a profit and always with the Put limiting the possible loss if the price of the stock collapses. An analysis of Case II, shows the possibility of several trades under the protection of the Call option. If the stock price declines to $17, the investor buys 100 shares on the market and delivers them to cover the short sale for a $300 profit. If the market price advances to the strike price or higher, he sells another 100 shares short, and so on—always protected by the Call.

CASE III—An investor has purchased 100 shares of ABC Company stock at $20, and the price advances to $30. A further advance is still possible, but the investor does not want to risk his handsome $1,000 profit without protecting it. He purchases a Put for insurance at $30 for a $400 premium. If the market price falls below $30, he can deliver his stock to the Put seller at $30 for a net profit of $600 ($1,000 gross profit less the $400 premium paid for the Put). On the other hand, the investor has bought courage with his Put, and can afford to speculate in complete confidence that the price will continue to advance beyond $30.

Federal income tax laws treat the acquisition of a Put as a short sale with special tax rules applying. Put buyers must be familiar with these rules. In general, profits realized with exercise of a Put are short-term and consequently taxed at ordinary income tax rates unless the stock delivered upon the exercise of the Put has been held more than six months before purchase of the Put and more of that stock has not been purchased after purchase of the Put.

CASE IV—An investor, feeling "bearish" about ABC Company, sells short 100 shares of its stock at $20. He feels so confident of his forecast that he does not purchase a Call for insurance as in Case II. The stock promptly advances to $25, but the investor, though shaken, feels that time will prove him right. Still, he does not want to risk a major loss, so he buys a six month and 10 day Call at a strike price of $25 for a $450 premium. If the stock goes higher, he has limited his additional loss to the cost of the premium, because during the life of the Call he can purchase stock at $25 to cover his short sale. This insurance enables him to maintain his position. If the stock price declines, he can recover the paper loss he incurred when the stock went from $20 to $25, and he may eventually make a profit. If he had purchased his Call at the same time he sold short, as in Case II, he would risk losing only the premium. With the purchase of the Call at $25, his total possible loss is $500 more. Moreover, with the stock at $25, he has probably paid a larger premium. In most cases, the higher the strike price, the larger the premium for a Call.

CASE V—A six month and 10 day Call has been purchased on ABC stock at $20. The price advances to $40 before the Call expires. The investor feels there is a reasonable chance that the stock will appreciate further, but he wants to secure the bulk of his profit. He does this by purchasing a Put at $40, to expire after his Call expires. His 20 point profit (less the premiums for the Call and Put) is guaranteed. Suppose the market price of the stock slips back to $30. The profit in the Call drops to $1,000, but there is now a $1,000 profit in the Put—less the premiums paid for both options.

CASE VI—With ABC stock at $40 an investor sells 100

shares short with the protection of a Call as in Case II. The stock plunges to $20 for a 20 point profit on the short sale, but instead of covering the short sale the investor buys a second Call, expiring shortly after the first. This is insurance in the hope that the stock will decline still further. Assuming the stock drops to $10, there is a 30 point profit in the short sale less the premiums for the two Calls which will both expire unexercised. If the price advances above $20 but is less than $40, the investor will let the first Call expire unexercised and exercise the second Call. If the price rises to $50, he will exercise both Calls. No matter how far above $20 the price of the stock advances, the profit of 20 points (less the premium for the two Calls) is guaranteed.

It is apparent from many examples in the above cases that an investor purchasing Puts and Calls may be best served by circumstances where his options expire unexercised. That investors should purchase options with no regret at their unexercised expiration is not generally appreciated. When used as insurance to maintain or develop favorable investment positions, this is exactly what the investor hopes for.

V

Mechanism of Stock Option Transactions

Option transactions usually involve a buyer and seller, their respective stockbrokers, and a Put and Call dealer.

Put and Call dealers represent firms whose business is to buy and sell stock options for profit. There are approximately twenty-five of these firms located in the New York financial district, varying in size and the extent of their activity in the business. They are not members of the major Stock Exchanges, and they earn no commissions on the purchase or sale of options. Their profit is the difference between the prices at which they buy and sell an option, and it varies for each transaction. The Put and Call dealers belong to the Put and Call Brokers and Dealers Association, which is a self-regulating body determining the rules of business activity for its members. The great degree of competition between dealers results in benefits for both option buyers and sellers by keeping the price of options reasonable for the buyer and attractive for the seller.

Mechanism of Stock Option Transactions

An option transaction begins when a potential buyer inquires about a particular option from his broker or directly from a Put and Call dealer. The broker, in turn, contacts a Put and Call dealer in New York to negotiate on behalf of his client. The broker earns nothing by completing the option, but takes his commission on the purchase and sale of stock if the option is exercised.

The potential option buyer may have seen an attractive option advertised in the financial newspapers by a Put and Call dealer. Or he may wish to negotiate a price for an option that he has not seen advertised but which he feels would be attractive. If the option is available, the dealer will quote a premium and the other terms of the contract directly to the customer, or to his broker. The customer may accept or reject the offer, or he may try to negotiate a lower premium perhaps by shortening the duration of the contract.

The Put and Call dealer will do his best to accommodate the customer, but he may not always be able to make the option available on the terms desired. If the option was advertised, it may already have been purchased by another customer. Or there may not be a seller available offering the specific option the buyer is seeking. If the price and terms of the option contract are satisfactory, the Put and Call dealer sells the contract to the option buyer and receives his premium in cash from the buyer or from his broker.

The Put and Call dealer may have sold his customer an option he had previously purchased from a seller. He may also have been negotiating simultaneously with a seller and buyer for prices that will assure him a reasonable profit. In some circumstances, especially on popular options commanding fairly well-established premiums, the dealer may sell an option that has not yet been sold to him by an option writer. He is confident that he can find an option writer willing to sell him the option at a price that allows him to make a profit.

To ensure that potential sellers of options are available to him, the Put and Call dealer may advertise in the financial papers the premiums he is willing to pay to option writers. If an option writer finds the Put and Call dealer's advertised offer attractive, he may ask his broker to contact the dealer to consummate the sale or he may arrange it himself. In any event a Stock Exchange member broker must be involved in the option sale to guarantee that the terms of the contract will be met by the option writer. Sometimes the Put and Call dealer will contact individual option writers directly if he feels that they may want to write a specific option, but again the option writer will refer the dealer to his broker to complete the transaction. Most of the time, the Put and Call dealer relies on his contacts with Stock Exchange member firms which have option departments to find writers for specific options.

Option writers also find attractive opportunities through Stock Exchange member firms which have option departments. These option brokers, as they are often called, receive $6.25 for arranging the sale of a Put or a Call, and $12.50 for arranging the sale of a Straddle. They only earn standard Stock Exchange commissions when stock is bought or sold as a result of the exercise of an option. (See the table of commissions at the end of this chapter.) Option writers tend to be active investors, buying and selling round lots of stock as options are exercised every two, three or six months. While they demand a great deal of service from their brokers, they are attractive customers with a high yield of commissions relative to invested capital.

The Put and Call dealer expects the fastest possible service from option brokers because his customer, the option buyer, wants to know as soon as possible if the transaction he has proposed will be completed. Often the option broker will have only minutes or at most, hours, to find an option seller. If the proposed transaction is presented to several

47

option brokers at once, the one who first finds a seller completes the transaction. If the option sale opportunity is attractive and a seller cannot be found immediately, the option broker may sell the option himself and transfer the sale to an option writer later. To successfully arrange option sales, the broker must know his customers, the particular stocks they are interested in, the types of options they favor, the degree of risk they are willing to take, and the amount of capital they usually have available. The author's experience with his own option broker has been that his broker knows the state of his account almost as well as the author himself. This is true despite the fact that the broker has several hundred customers.

Put and Call dealers and option brokers have some of the most demanding jobs in the securities business. Each dealer or broker daily handles hundreds of inquiries and completes hundreds of transactions involving enormous sums of money. Friendly and courteous as the individual desires to be, he has no more than a very limited time for discussion. As he talks to one customer, invariably the phone rings in the background demanding immediate attention. Communications are his major problem. He must have the time and means to contact his customers, whether buyers or sellers, wherever they happen to be.

Many offers to buy options remain valid for one to several hours. Some, however, require almost instantaneous negotiation. Once the option broker offers terms and premium for a specific option, he expects the option writer to quickly accept, reject, or offer an alternative bid. The option writer cannot hesitate, because there may be other writers anxious to accept the bid. Some very active option writers have "hot line" phones direct to their broker's desk. Others authorize their broker to conclude option sales on a particular stock without further consultation—the strike price, premium, and time limit having been specified beforehand. If the option writer wishes, he can authorize his broker to conclude transactions at his discretion within even wider limits.

Most option buyers purchase Calls. Most option writers, attracted by the larger premiums, prefer writing Straddles. Put and Call dealers have developed what they call a "conversion" to satisfy both buyers and writers. The conversion allows the dealer to purchase a Straddle and convert the Put component into a Call for sale. Here is an example of the conversion:

A Put and Call dealer receives an inquiry for ten six month and 10 day Calls on ABC Company stock. The potential buyer is willing to pay a premium of $400 for each Call at a strike price of $20. The dealer calls option writers he knows, or an option broker, offering let us say a premium of $325 for a Call and $525 for a Straddle. He finds he is able to purchase four of the ten Calls at $325. These he sells directly to the customer for $400 each. The dealer also buys three Straddles (three Calls and three Puts) from an option writer at $525 each. Seven of the ten Calls are now available to the buyer. The dealer now calls his "conversion house," a Stock Exchange member firm, and asks them to convert the three Puts into three Calls. The conversion house does this by receiving the three Puts from the dealer, issuing him three Calls and buying 300 shares of ABC stock in the market at $20 as security, thus completing the order for ten Calls. The conversion is risk free to the conversion house and to the Put and Call dealer (the latter being a middleman between the conversion house and the option writer). If the Calls are exercised, the conversion house delivers the 300 shares at their purchase price of $20 to the buyer. If the Calls are not exercised, the conversion house puts the 300 shares at their strike price of $20 to the option writer.

The conversion house passes on the costs of the conver-

49

Mechanism of Stock Option Transactions

sion to the Put and Call dealer. The use of the conversion house money tied up in purchasing 300 shares of ABC Company stock on the open market is charged at reasonable rates geared to current bank rates. Nine or ten percent is charged currently (1968). The interest rates are calculated for the full term of the option contract and are not refunded if the Calls are exercised before expiration. Certain "floor" brokerage fees and taxes are also involved in the purchase and sale of the stock. A table of these fees appears at the end of this chapter.

In the example above, the conversion house might charge $100 interest on the money used to buy each lot of 100 shares of ABC Company stock that was used as security for each Call delivered to the Put and Call dealer. The conversion house also charges the dealer $7.30 in "floor" brokerage fees and $5.00 in taxes. The total cost of converting one Put to one Call is, then, $112.30. The dealer pays this sum to the conversion house when the conversion is completed and the Call is issued. The dealer thus paid $525 to the option writer for each Straddle, a $12.50 fee to the option broker for handling the transaction, and $112.30 to the conversion house for converting each Put into a Call. Thus he has paid approximately $650 and has two Calls to show for it. Since the dealer received $800 in premiums for the two Calls, he has realized a profit of about $75 for each Call, or about the same amount as for the straight sale of a Call.

If the Calls are exercised before the expiration date of the option contract, the conversion house enjoys as additional profit the difference between the interest charges paid by the Put and Call dealer and the amount the house used to maintain the 300 shares of stock until delivery. The conversion house has a further possibility for profit in the above situation if the stock price falls below the strike price after the Calls are exercised but while the three Puts the house holds are still valid. In this case, the house will buy 300 shares of stock on the market at the depressed price and put them to the option writer at the strike price of $20.

Below is a diagram illustrating the lines of communication between the people and organizations involved in completing an option transaction.

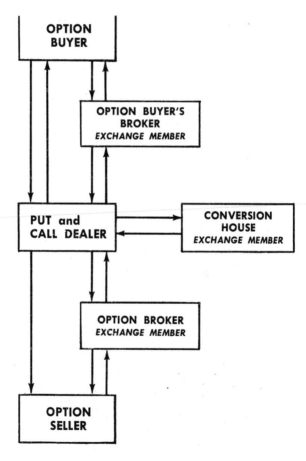

Mechanism of Stock Option Transactions

FLOOR BROKERAGE FEES FOR CONVERSIONS

MARKET PRICE OF STOCK	NEW YORK STOCK EXCHANGE $ AMOUNT	AMERICAN STOCK EXCHANGE $ AMOUNT
1–2	2.50	3.50
2–5	2.80	4.10
5–10	4.20	6.60
10–20	6.20	8.00
20–40	7.30	10.20
40–100	7.70	11.30
100–150	8.70	13.00

TAXES FOR CONVERSIONS

MARKET PRICE OF STOCK	$ AMOUNT
under 10	2.50
10–19⅞	3.75
20 and over	5.00

NEW YORK AND AMERICAN STOCK EXCHANGE COMMISSIONS

Round Lots (100 shares)

VALUE OF TRANSACTION	COMMISSION
Under $100	negotiated
100–399	2% of value of transaction plus $3.00
400–2,399	1% plus $7.00
2,400–4,999	½% plus $19.00
5,000 and above	⅒% plus $39.00

Odd Lots (Less than 100 shares)

Same commissions as above, less $2.00, with a minimum of $6.00 for a single transaction. When stock is purchased, an odd-lot differential is added to the round-lot market price. When stock is sold, the odd-lot differential is subtracted from the round-lot market price. The purchase or sale price of an odd lot includes the differential.

New York Stock Exchange

Round-lot Market Price	*Odd-lot Differential*
54⅞ or below	⅛ point
55 or above	¼ point

American Stock Exchange

Round-lot Market Price	*Odd-lot Differential*
39⅞ or below	⅛ point
40 or above	¼ point

VI

Profits in Selling Stock Options

The incentive for selling stock options is the opportunity to earn an attractive return on investment for a given level of risk. In each case the maximum profit that can be realized by the option writer until the option is exercised or expires is the premium he has received. The premium is, of course, a vital consideration. It must, however, be related to the investment required and the duration of that investment.

To increase the return on his investment, the option writer uses "margin" money borrowed from his broker. The amount of money he can borrow is strictly regulated by the Securities and Exchange Commission and the Stock Exchanges. From 1963 until June, 1968, the basic margin requirement was 70%. In June, 1968, the margin requirement was raised to 80%. This means that to buy stock in the market a minimum of 80% of the purchase price of the stock must be paid in cash, and up to 20% can be borrowed from a broker. A minimum of $2,000 in equity (cash, stock, bonds, etc.) is required to open a margin account. All stock on which margin money is borrowed must be kept in a margin account and in the broker's possession. Option writers must maintain margin accounts which allow their option broker to execute transactions they have written without contacting the option writer for permission. These margin accounts must be maintained regardless of whether "margin" money has been used.

The use of margin money is usually associated in the public mind with a risk that is higher than it is prudent to take. But option writers almost universally use margin because it involves a different level of risk than for the conventional investor. The option writer is protected against adverse stock price changes by the amount of the premium he has received for sale of the option. Margin money is borrowed from brokers at 7% to 8% depending on existing bank rates. A successful option program should yield a much higher return on invested capital, so that it makes good sense to borrow. In option writing, margin rules substantially affect the investment required to sustain the program, and they are discussed in detail in Chapter IX. For purposes of evaluating the return on investment for an individual option sale, the following basic rules should be understood.

Margin Rule for a Call

To write a Call option when the market price and the strike price are identical, a minimum of 30% of the market price in cash is required. Alternatively, 100 shares of stock can be placed in the margin account as security. During the life of the Call, 100 shares of stock are adequate security regardless of the price of the stock. If cash alone is used as security, the general margin requirement during the life of the Call (and initially, if the market and strike prices are different) is 30% of the market price plus the market price minus the strike price.

Margin Rule for a Put

To write a Put option when the market and the strike prices are identical, a minimum of 25% of the market price, in cash, must be deposited in the margin account. However, if a Put is sold against a short position, there is no minimum cash requirement. During the life of the Put (and initially, if the strike and market prices are different) the general margin requirement is 25% of the market price plus the strike price minus the market price.

Margin Rule for a Straddle

To write a Straddle, and during its life, cash security is required for only one of the two options (the Put or the Call) —whichever option requires the larger cash security according to the rules above. If 100 shares of stock are used as security for the Call portion of the Straddle, the option writer must still put up cash to secure the Put. If one of

the options is exercised, margin security for the remaining
Put or Call will be as above.

Margin Rules for Strips, Straps and Spreads

Initially, and during their life, the security required for a
Strip is the same as for a Straddle and a Put; for a *Strap*
the same as for a Straddle and a Call; for a *Spread* whichever is larger, the Put or Call requirement, plus the initial
difference between the market and strike prices in accordance with the general margin requirement for the Put and
Call.

The cash requirements cited above are the minimum.
Individual option brokers may require more cash security
especially for new option-writing accounts or for writers
engaged in high-risk programs. Because the option broker
must guarantee that the option writer's contracts will be
honored, he is justified in requiring perhaps more than the
minimum margin security.

As stated above, the option writer should weigh the potential return on his investment in the sale of an option against
the risks involved. The evaluation of the risks is subjective
and involves many factors which could adversely affect the
price of the stock (see Chapter VII). The potential percent
annual return on investment, however, can be calculated
precisely. The method of calculation varies with the option
sold. The general formula is:

$$\frac{\text{Percent Return}}{\text{on Investment}} = \frac{(\text{premium} - \text{costs})(\text{days in year})(100)}{(\text{cash required})(\text{life of option in days})}$$

Summarized below are formulas for calculating the potential annual percent return on investment for sales of Puts, Calls and Straddles, assuming an 80% margin requirement and assuming that if the options are exercised, they are not exercised before expiration.

The factors involved and their designation in the formulas are:

R = Percent return per year on cash investment required.

P = Premium—the premium received by the option writer, which can be used as part of his cash requirement.

C = Margin costs—the interest cost for borrowing margin money.

B = Brokerage fees—the brokerage fees which must be paid by the option writer upon exercise of the option.

S = Strike price × 100 shares in cash.

D = Life of the option in days.

M = Market price at the time option is written × 100 shares in cash.

1. *Sale of a Call with 100 shares of stock as security*

$$R = \frac{(P - C - B)\,(36{,}500)}{(0.8M - P)D}$$

2. *Sale of a Call with minimum cash as security*

$$R = \frac{(P)\,(36{,}500)}{[0.3M + (M - S) - P]D}$$

3. *Sale of a Put with minimum cash as security*

$$R = \frac{(P)\,(36{,}500)}{[0.25M + (S - M) - P]D}$$

4. *Sale of a Straddle with 100 shares of stock as security*

$$R = \frac{(P - C - B)\,(36{,}500)}{[1.05M + (S - M) - P]D}$$

Profits in Selling Stock Options

5. *Sale of a Straddle with minimum cash as security*

$$R = \frac{(P - B)(36,500)}{[0.3M + (M - S) - P]D}$$ when M is greater than S or M = S

$$R = \frac{(P - B)(36,500)}{[0.25M + (S - M) - P]D}$$ when S is greater than M

Below are examples of various types of option sales, their margin and cash requirements, and their annual percent return on investment:

CASE I—An option writer sells a six month and 10 day Call on ABC stock at $20 for a premium of $300. He purchases 100 shares of the stock at $20, thinking it likely that the price will rise and the Call will be exercised during the life of the contract or at expiration. If the option expires unexercised, the market price will be below $20, the option writer will continue to hold the stock, and the premium will be his profit. He purchased the stock at what he considered an attractive price and can wait for it to recover in price, or he can sell another option with the same stock as security.

An option writer could also buy 100 shares of a stock at what he considers a good price and sell a Call on it only after the price advances to a strike price higher than his purchase price. His potential profit, if the stock is called, is the premium plus the difference between the strike price and his purchase price. For example, the option buyer may have purchased 100 shares of ABC at $15. He holds it until the price reaches $20, and then sells a Call. His profit, on exercise, is $500 plus the premium.

The risk in selling a Call with 100 shares of stock as security is not great. In the Case above, the price of the stock has only to rise above $20 at expiration for the option to be exercised and the $300 premium (less costs) to be enjoyed as profit. Even if the stock price falls to $17, the option writer still breaks even if he sells his stock. At prices below $17, the option writer can sell his stock at any time knowing that he is losing $300 less than the investor who had bought at $20 in the market, without the cushion of a premium. If the stock appreciates to $30 during the life of the option, the option writer would have made a larger profit by holding the stock rather than selling a Call on it. On the other hand, the option writer is satisfied with his return, realizing that his risk of losing money on the transaction has been less than that incurred by the option buyer, and even less than that of the conventional investor buying the same stock at the same price in the market and waiting for the price to rise.

When the option writer bought 100 shares of ABC stock at $20 as security for the sale of the Call (strike price also at $20), he had to pay $1,600 in cash, according to the 80% margin rules. Receiving the premium of $300 has reduced this to $1,300. The remaining 20%, or $400, of the stock price he can borrow from his broker. The option writer computes the interest charges on that loan at 7%, or $14, for the six month and 10 day life of the option. If the stock is called before expiration of the contract, the interest charges will be correspondingly lower, and the percent return on the investment somewhat higher. Brokerage fees for the purchase and sale of the stock at $20, assuming the stock is called, will be $54. The percent return on the investment can be computed as follows:

$$R = \frac{(P - C - B)\,(36,500)}{(0.8M - P)D} = \frac{(300 - 14 - 54)\,(36,500)}{(1600 - 300)(193)}$$

$$R = 33.8$$

CASE II—An option writer sells a six month and 10 day Call on ABC stock at $20 for a premium of $300. The market price and strike price are identical. He thinks the stock is over-priced and will fall below the strike price by expiration. During the life of the option he does not expect the market price to rise far enough above the strike price to tempt the buyer to exercise his option. He has sold a "naked" or unprotected option. If the Call is exercised, the option writer must purchase stock in the market for delivery. If the market price of the stock is, in fact, below the strike price at expiration and the stock has not been called, the option will expire and the premium will be his profit. If the market price advances to $23 when the Call is exercised, the option writer's premium covers him, and he breaks even. Beyond this price, the option writer is in the position of a short seller, and there is no theoretical limit to his potential loss. Moreover, as the stock advances, the cash security required by the broker increases according to the margin rules.

Here is a calculation of the annual percent return on the investment. The cash security required by the margin rules is 30% of the market price, plus the difference, if any, between the market and the strike prices. There is no margin money borrowed, and there are no brokerage fees because there has been no purchase of stock.

$$R = \frac{(P)(36,500)}{[0.3M + (M - S) - P]D} = \frac{(300)(36,500)}{(600 + 0 - 300)(193)}$$

$$R = 189$$

The percent return on investment is very large. So are the risks in selling naked or unprotected Calls. Option writers should be extremely hesitant in undertaking such transactions. There are circumstances, however, when an option writer may hedge his position by selling a Call protected by fifty shares of stock, or by selling two Calls, one protected and one naked. In these situations, the percent yearly return on investment is between that realized in Cases I and II, while the cash investment required is less than in Case I and more than in Case II. This hedge position can be varied according to the degree of risk an option writer will tolerate. A relatively low level of risk may be three protected and one naked Call, or perhaps one Call protected by seventy-five shares. A high level of risk may be one protected Call and three naked Calls, or twenty-five shares protecting one Call.

CASE III—An option writer sells a 95-day Put on ABC stock at $20 for a premium of $150. The market price and the strike price are identical. He expects that upon expiration the market price of the stock will exceed the strike price. However, he will not be dismayed if he is put the stock and must pay $20 for it because he felt positive about ABC stock when he wrote the Put. Moreover, the $150 premium he received has effectively reduced the purchase price to $18½. It is a curious fact that the demand for Puts is greatest after severe market declines, near the bottom of a market cycle. This is perhaps explained by speculators expecting further price declines, or investors purchasing stock and buying Puts simultaneously for protection. Whatever the reason, the option writer is in a good position to take advantage of the demand.

A calculation of percent yearly return on investment is presented below. The cash security required by margin rules is 25% of the market price. The cash premium may be applied as part of this. Interest charges on margin money borrowed for stock and brokerage fees are not applicable because the option writer has not purchased stock.

$$R = \frac{(P)(36{,}500)}{[0.25M + (S - M) - P]D} = \frac{(150)(36{,}500)}{(500 + 0 - 150)(95)}$$

$$R = 165$$

The return in Case III is certainly very attractive, but the option writer must consider one other aspect. Money must be available to purchase the stock if it is put. If the money is not available, the stock must be simultaneously purchased and sold on the market for a loss at perhaps a depressed price. The prudent option writer will earmark funds for purchasing the stock simultaneously with the sale of the Put. The reserved funds should be considered as part of the cash commitment required for the transaction in order to bring the risk to an acceptable level. Instead of the minimum of 25% of the market price (less the premium) required for the cash security, the option writer should consider 80% of the strike price (less the premium) as his cash commitment. A recalculation of the return would then be:

$$R = \frac{(P)\,(36{,}500)}{(0.80S - P)\,(D)} = \frac{(150)\,(36{,}500)}{(1600 - 150)\,(95)}$$

$$R = 39.8$$

The cash represented above by 80% of the strike price (less the premium) will be used to purchase the stock if it is put. If the stock advances in price to where the option writer feels confident that the option will expire unexercised, he can reinvest his cash in another transaction. The more cash that is considered released, the more the return is increased. The minimum cash requirement must, of course, always be maintained according to the general margin rule for a Put discussed above.

CASE IV—An option writer sells a one-year Straddle on ABC stock at $20 for a premium of $750. The market price and strike price are identical. He protects the Call option of the Straddle with purchase of 100 shares of stock, for he feels confident that the stock price will rise and the Call will be exercised. In this case, his profit will be the $750 premium (less costs), assuming the Put has expired unexercised. But if the market price falls below the strike price, the Put will be exercised and the option writer will own 200 shares—

the 100 held as security for the Call and the 100 shares put. In the case above, the break-even point is $16¼ if the stock is sold. Below this, the loss on liquidation will increase at twice the rate of selling the individual Put or Call because twice as many shares are involved. The higher premiums paid for Straddles are the option writer's incentive to assume this level of risk. Most option writers readily engage in this type of transaction. Indeed, perhaps the majority of options sold are Straddles in which the option writer maintains 100 shares of stock as security for the Call portion of the Straddle.

Here is the percent yearly return on investment in Case IV: The purchase of 100 shares of ABC stock satisfies the margin requirement for the Call portion of the Straddle. And those shares themselves can be bought on margin, $1,600 in cash being required. The margin requirement for the Put is 25% of the market price in cash, or an additional $500. The total cash requirement of $2,100 is reduced by the $750 premium to $1,350. To complete the stock purchase, the option writer need not borrow margin money from his broker. The brokerage fees for the purchase and expected sale of the stock on exercise of the Call are $54.

$$R = \frac{(P - C - B)\ (36{,}500)}{[1.05M + (S - M) - P]D} = \frac{(750 - 0 - 54)\ (36{,}500)}{(2100 + 0 - 750)(365)}$$

$$R = 51.5$$

As in Case III, the prudent option writer will maintain a cash reserve of $1,400 for purchase of the necessary stock on margin should the Put be exercised. This cash reserve should be taken into account in computing the percent yearly return on the transaction. In practice, however, the option writer will not necessarily establish the reserve until late in the life of the Straddle, and only then if it becomes likely that the Put will be exercised. Most Puts are held by

Profits in Selling Stock Options

conversion houses and most conversion houses, for maximum security, do not exercise them until expiration.

CASE V—An option writer sells a six month and 10 day Straddle on ABC stock at $20 for a premium of $500. The market price and strike price are identical. He feels that the stock will decline and that the Put will eventually be exercised. The option writer prefers to risk selling a naked Straddle where the Call option is unprotected by 100 shares of stock. If the stock is called, the option writer must buy it in the market. Above a price of $25 he will suffer a loss on the overall transaction, taking into account the $500 premium received. On the other hand, if the stock is put, only the potential loss associated with the stock put need be considered. For example, the whole position can be liquidated by sale of the stock put to the option writer down to a price of $15 before loss results. Had the Put been exercised when the option writer was already holding 100 shares of stock to protect his Call, his potential losses would have doubled. His breakeven point on liquidation would be $17½ per share, and at $15, he would lose his premium and an additional $500.

There are circumstances in which an option writer may consider the sale of a naked Straddle. He may have previously sold a Put or a Straddle at a strike price higher than the current market price, and he expects the stock to be put. This stock could then become his security for writing a new Straddle. Or the option writer may sell a naked Straddle expecting the market price of the stock to decline during the life of the contract. He intends then to buy stock security for the Straddle at the lower price.

Here is a calculation of the yearly percent return on the Straddle cited above: Margin rules require the option writer to put up in cash the greater of the two amounts required for an individual Put or Call—in this case 30% of the market price, or $600 for the Call. The $500 premium will reduce this to $100 in cash investment. Brokerage fees will amount to about $50 upon exercise of either the Put or the Call when the position is liquidated.

$$R = \frac{(P - B)(36,500)}{[0.3M + (M - S) - P]D} = \frac{(500 - 50)(36,500)}{(600 + 0 - 500)(193)}$$

$$R = 850$$

The return calculated above has only limited significance. There is little possibility of netting the premium as profit with the almost negligible extra cash requirement. Such a situation will result only if the market price of the stock is the same or very close to the strike price at expiration and the options have not been exercised in the meantime. Occasionally this will happen. But usually the option writer will write such a Straddle expecting the stock to fluctuate narrowly near the strike price. With the market price between $15 and $25, exercise of either option will result in profit. The closer the market price and the strike price at time of exercise of either option, the larger will be the option writer's profit.

The premiums charged for Straddles often cover most, if not all, of the minimum cash security requirement for the Straddle. But the substantial potential profits in Case V are associated with all the risks described in selling a naked Call and the loss that could result if the Put is exercised and the market price declines substantially from the strike price. In fact, the option writer will engage in the kind of transaction cited in Case V expecting to realize, at best, only a part of the premium as profit. Moreover, if the stock fluctuates above or below the strike price during the life of the contract, margin rules will force the option writer to increase his cash investment. Sometimes, option writers offset the risks and potential profits of the Call portion of the Straddle by purchasing some stock. In Case V, for example, 50 shares of ABC stock could have been bought simultaneously with the sale of the Straddle. Option writers occasionally write Calls and Straddles without purchasing the stock involved but owning an equivalent security as protection. For example, an option writer may have purchased a Call which has value as a result of increase in the price of the stock. He may then sell a Call or Straddle on the same stock expiring before his original Call expires, using his original Call as security. If the option buyer exercises his Call or the Call portion of the Straddle, the option writer exercises his original Call and delivers that stock to the option buyer. Even though he owns a Call, the option writer must maintain the minimum cash security when writing the Call or Straddle.

The option writer can also protect himself by owning convertible bonds—(bonds which yield interest and can be converted to a specified number of shares of common stock). In this case, if a Call or Straddle is exercised because the price of the stock has risen, the bonds may also have increased in market value by an equivalent amount. The bonds could then be converted to common stock and delivered to the buyer who has exercised his option. The option writer may also retain his bonds and purchase stock in the market for delivery. He will purchase the stock at a higher price and sell at the strike price. But the convertible bonds may have increased proportionately in value, so that there will be no loss on the overall transaction. Ownership of convertible bonds does not eliminate the necessity of maintaining the minimum cash security for Straddles or Calls. Only ownership of the actual stock on which the option is written eliminates the necessity of cash as security.

Option writers owning warrants on a given stock can sell options on that stock, using the warrants as security. A warrant is the right to purchase one share, or a number of shares, of common stock at a specified price usually over an extended period of time. Warrants are like Calls, differing only in their extended life and the fact that they can be purchased in odd lots. The market price of a warrant usually advances along with the price of the associated common stock. If a Call is exercised, the option writer can buy the stock in the market and deliver it to the option buyer. The warrant is his protection because it will have increased in price as much, or almost as much, as the common stock. Since warrants usually cost less, and in many cases considerably less than the associated common stock, the option writer can enjoy a higher percent return because his cash investment in the warrants is less than it would be in the equivalent common stock. The protection of warrants is not absolute. There is no guarantee that they will advance in price exactly in proportion to the common stock. However, it is reasonable to assume that their respective prices will move at least in the same direction. In accordance with margin rules, minimum cash as security must be maintained in the absence of ownership of the common stock.

In the preceding pages, mathematical formulas have been presented for calculating the yearly percent return on the sale of Calls, Puts and Straddles. The option writer should understand the derivation of these formulas and be able to use them to calculate the annual percent return for any proposed option sale.

At the end of this chapter we have included two sets of graphs to enable the option seller to determine the annual percent return for the most common options. The graphs are for 95-day and six month and 10 day options, and they cover the sale of Calls and Straddles with 100 shares of stock as security, and the sale of Puts with minimum cash as security.

Profits in Selling Stock Options

The following assumptions have been made in preparing the graphs:

1. The margin requirement for the purchase of stock is 80% of the market price in cash.
2. The general margin requirements for the sale of Puts, Calls and Straddles are as stated on Pages 56 and 57.
3. The market price of the stock and the strike price are identical when the option is sold.
4. The interest rate charged for margin money is 7%.
5. Brokerage fees for the sale and purchase of 100 shares or "round" lots, are at the Stock Exchange Commission's current (1968) rates.

Changes in assumptions 1 and 2 will make the graphs obsolete. If the margin requirements for stock purchases are changed from 80%, for example, the Call and Straddle graphs must be changed accordingly. The Put graphs are not affected since stock purchase is not involved in computing the potential annual percent return on investment. New graphs can be prepared with the aid of the formulas modified by the changed margin requirements. With the new formula assume a constant percent return per year, and for different strike prices calculate the resulting premium and plot the graph. Following the same procedure for different percent returns per year will result in a "family" of curves. Small changes in assumptions 4 or 5 will not materially affect the relationships presented in the graphs. If the market price and the strike price are different when the Call or Straddle option is sold, an adjustment can be made: If the strike price is greater than the market price, add the difference between the two prices to the premium. If the strike price is lower than the market price, subtract that difference from the premium. Plot the adjusted premiums on the graph and proceed as outlined below.

In the graphs, the annual percent return for a Call or a Straddle with stock as security is based on the assumption that the stock is called at expiration. For the percent return on the Put, it is assumed that the contract expires unexercised.

Any profits or losses realized on a given stock before the sale of the option should be considered a separate transaction. The percent return per year on the proposed option should be based only on the premium, the market price of the stock at the time the option is offered, and the strike price if it differs from the market price. The history of ownership of the stock may, of course, play a part in determining the attractiveness of the proposed option. The length of time a stock has been held, for example, will affect its taxable status.

The use of the graphs is quite simple. In the proposed option sale the premium and the strike price (which in most cases is the market price) are specified. The premium is read on the vertical axis, and the strike price is read on the horizontal axis. The premium and the strike price will meet on or between two of the "family" of curves representing a constant percent return per year. Each curve is numbered with the corresponding annual percent return (called "R"). If the premium and strike price meet between two curves, draw a vertical line through the point of meeting and determine how far it is from the two curves. For example, if the point of meeting is 30% of the distance between R = 40 and R = 50, the percent yearly return on the proposed option will be 43.

The maximum strike price on the graphs is $70. They can be used, however, for options in which the strike price is much higher. For example, to evaluate an option in which the premium is $1,000 and the strike price is $120, divide both the premium and the strike price by two and read the percent return per year for $500 and $60 respectively. This procedure is valid because the curves in the upper ranges are almost straight lines.

The two sets of graphs can be used to roughly estimate the much rarer 65-day and one-year options. The yearly percent return on a 65-day option will be almost 50% greater than that on a 95-day option for the same strike price and premium. The percent return on a one-year option will be about 50% less than that on a six month and 10 day option at the same terms.

However, it must be emphasized that these percentages are only approximate and, especially in the lower ranges of the curves, they are liable to serious error. The basic formulas should be used wherever possible to calculate options for time spans not covered by the graphs.

Two unexpected conclusions emerge from a study of the graphs.

1. For every increase in the premium, there is more than a proportional increase in the percent return per year. A 50% increase in the premium for a particular option will often result in a 100% increase in the yearly percent return.

This is true for several reasons. A larger premium means a larger potential profit and a decrease in the amount of extra cash required for an investment. More important, brokerage fees and the interest rate on borrowed margin money are the same no matter what the premium. Once these costs are covered, the increased premium is applied directly to the profits.

2. The premium for a 95-day Call or Straddle is usually about ⅔ that for a corresponding six month and 10 day option. It would seem on the surface that the 95-day option will yield a substantially higher percent return per year since the contract is in force for only half as long, but the premium is only ⅓ smaller. The graphs show that this is

not the case: The 95-day option yields only a marginally better overall return than the six month and 10 day contract.

The reason is again the fixed costs of an option transaction. They represent a higher percentage of the premium in the 95-day option than they do in the six month and 10 day contract.

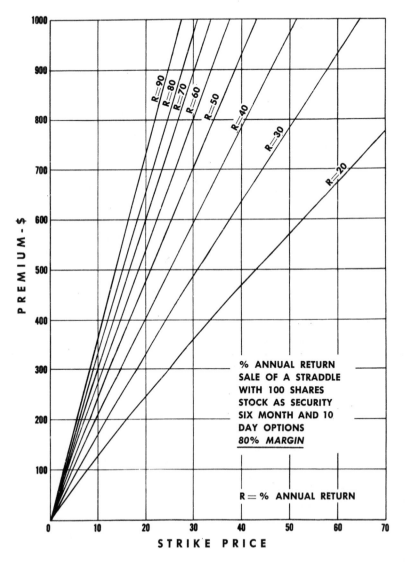

% ANNUAL RETURN
SALE OF A STRADDLE
WITH 100 SHARES
STOCK AS SECURITY
SIX MONTH AND 10
DAY OPTIONS
80% MARGIN

R = % ANNUAL RETURN

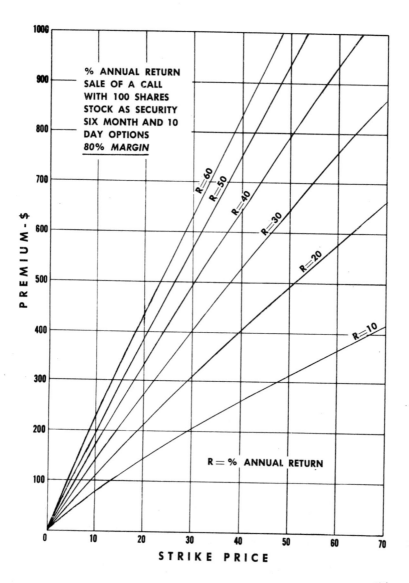

% ANNUAL RETURN
SALE OF A CALL
WITH 100 SHARES
STOCK AS SECURITY
SIX MONTH AND 10
DAY OPTIONS
80% MARGIN

R = % ANNUAL RETURN

PREMIUM - $

STRIKE PRICE

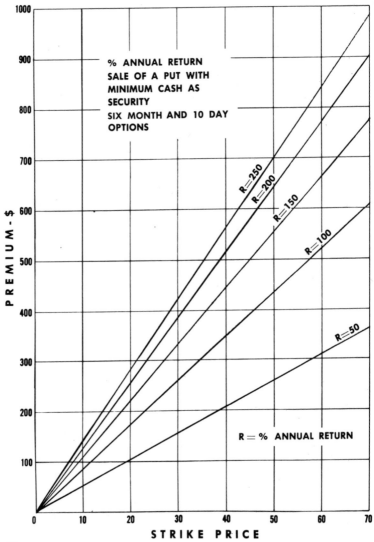

% ANNUAL RETURN
SALE OF A PUT WITH
MINIMUM CASH AS
SECURITY
SIX MONTH AND 10 DAY
OPTIONS

R=250
R=200
R=150
R=100
R=50

R = % ANNUAL RETURN

PREMIUM - $

STRIKE PRICE

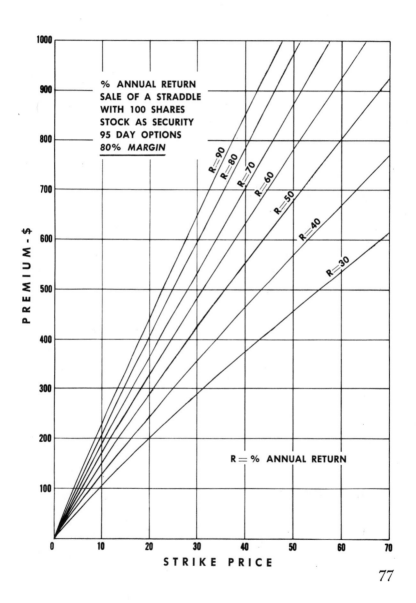

% ANNUAL RETURN
SALE OF A STRADDLE
WITH 100 SHARES
STOCK AS SECURITY
95 DAY OPTIONS
80% MARGIN

R = % ANNUAL RETURN

PREMIUM - $

STRIKE PRICE

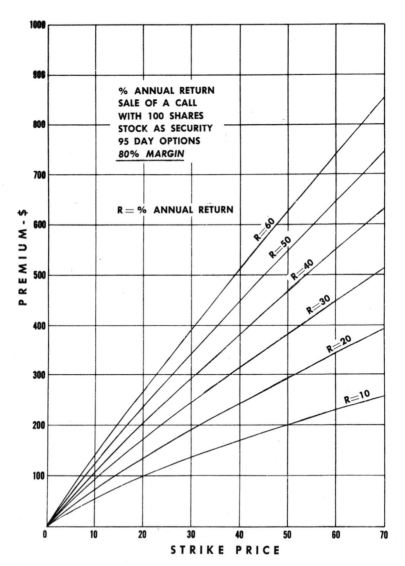

% ANNUAL RETURN
SALE OF A CALL
WITH 100 SHARES
STOCK AS SECURITY
95 DAY OPTIONS
80% MARGIN

R = % ANNUAL RETURN

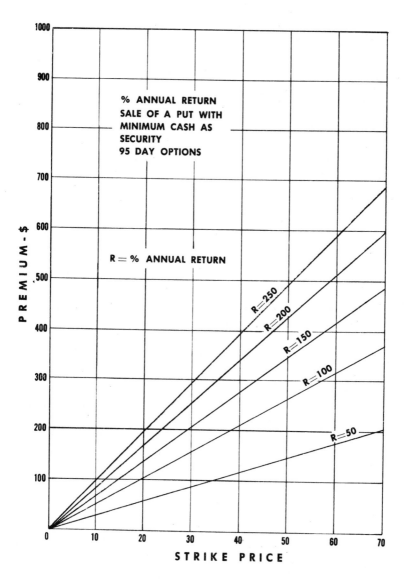

% ANNUAL RETURN
SALE OF A PUT WITH
MINIMUM CASH AS
SECURITY
95 DAY OPTIONS

R = % ANNUAL RETURN

R=250
R=200
R=150
R=100
R=50

PREMIUM - $

STRIKE PRICE

VII

Risks in Selling Stock Options

The potential profits in stock-option selling can be evaluated quantitatively, as illustrated in the preceding chapter. However, these potential profits must be balanced against the definite risk that the option will not work out as hoped for. The evaluation of these risks is *subjective* rather than quantitative and depends on the experience, skill, and knowledge of the option writer. The risks will vary both with the type of option sold and with the particular stock involved. The risks must be evaluated realistically for every option transaction, and the success of this evaluation will determine the success of the investment program. The option writer has considerable flexibility in choosing the risk levels he is willing to tolerate. He must, however, be absolutely realistic when he considers his capacity to appraise and tolerate risk. Inevitably, the highest percent returns per year on invested capital will be enjoyed by option writers in high-risk programs which are most skillfully executed. However, hand-

Risks in Selling Stock Options

some profits can be enjoyed by option writers with relatively low-risk programs requiring less skill and experience in execution.

The evaluation of the risks in a proposed option sale begins with the evaluation of the stock involved and its probable future action in the market. In sales of Puts, and Calls and Straddles with stock as security, the option writer will realize his maximum profit if the market price of the stock is at or above the strike price at expiration. Only in the very high-risk situation of selling naked options will the option writer benefit if the market price declines below the strike price at expiration. With the exception of naked options, the lowest level of risk will be associated with those stocks most resistant to market price declines in the opinion of the option writer. In the case of market price declines, the sale of a Straddle with 100 shares of stock as security is more risky than the sale of an individual Put or Call.

Except when selling naked options, possession of stock by the option writer is always involved—stock held as security in the sale of a Call or a Straddle; stock that he must be ready to buy at the strike price in the case of a Put. Thus he must consider all the factors that a conventional investor considers before buying an attractive stock: Price-earnings ratio, future earnings potential, previous market history, and general market prospects.

Option writers and conventional investors differ in this respect, however. The conventional investor may be willing to risk substantial stock price declines while he waits for the price appreciation wherein his profit lies. By contrast, option writers' profits on optioned stock are at a maximum as long as the market price does not fall below the strike price. The safest stocks for option writers will be those which appear least subject to market price declines.

Option writers often discover attractive option sale situations through the stock advisory services commonly used by conventional investors. But while the conventional investor will be disappointed in the advisory service's recommendation if the stock price does not rise substantially in a reasonable time, the option writer will not necessarily be dismayed. In fact, the option writer may have held many stocks for a substantial period and written many profitable options on them without the stocks themselves having appreciated significantly. If, on the other hand, the advisory service is correct and the stock price does rise, the option writer is content with his fixed profit.

These factors should be considered when evaluating the risk of price declines in any stock proposed for an option sale:

Price-Earnings Ratio—The lower the price-earnings ratio the greater will be the resistance of the stock to price declines. Ratios between 10:1 and 15:1 indicate that current earnings should be a stabilizing factor in the price of the stock. Conversely, ratios above 20:1 suggest that factors other than current earnings are contributing to the price of the stock. Stocks with a high price-earnings ratio may subsequently fall out of favor with investors resulting in market price declines.

Recent Earnings History—Projecting future earnings from the history of recent earnings is useful in estimating probable future market action of the stock. Stable or rising quarterly earnings will tend to be a stabilizing influence on market price. Substantial fluctuations in quarterly earnings may forecast a volatile market price.

High-Low Price Range for Year—If, during the year, the highest market price of a stock is more than double the lowest market price (a ratio of 2:1 or more), this is indicative of a volatile stock. The risk may be especially high if the option sale is being considered near the high for the year. Ratios below 1.5:1 are indicative of relative market price stability which may be projected into the near-term future.

Company Sales per Share of Common Stock—A high ratio of company sales per share of common stock—$30 per share and above—is characteristic of some very volatile stocks. For example, a stock with a market price of $15 and company sales of $50 per share could be much more volatile than a $15 stock with company sales of $10 per share. Such high ratios simply imply a relatively small number of common shares outstanding or a "thin" market. Comparatively small changes in the company's percent earnings on sales can be reflected in substantial changes in earnings per share and equivalent fluctuations in the market price of the stock. When the percent earnings on sales decline in stock with a thin market, the risk of market price declines is substantial. A ratio of company sales per share of common stock below 20:1 will tend to show less severe fluctuations of earnings per share with changes in the company's percent earnings on sales. A high ratio of bonds and preferred stock to common stock, or a small percentage of common stock in public hands, are also indicative of a thin market and consequent volatility.

Chart History of Stocks—Charts analyzing the long and short term price history of stocks are very useful tools in estimating the risk of a price decline. These charts can be obtained from brokers or from charting services. Basic chart analysis will indicate the general price trend of the stock both short and long-term. They may also show price decline resistance or "support" points which may be considered reassuring. A well defined upward or steady trend of the stock price will indicate a lower level of price decline risk.

Some option writers enjoy conspicuous success selling options on stocks with unusually depressed prices. These stocks are characterized by very low earnings or even by losses, a book value per share perhaps greater than the market price, and generally unfavorable market performance for a substantial period of time. Stock price charts often suggest the existence of a "floor" near which the stock exhibits strong resistance to price decline. Selling options near the "floor" price is a very attractive situation for the option writer. Before committing himself, the option writer should, of course, assure himself that the financial health of the company is basically sound. There is often a lively demand for options on these depressed issues, perhaps because the possibility of improved company performance and subsequent investment favor attracts option buyers hoping for substantial percent price increases.

In addition to evaluating the factors above, the option writer should consider the probable general course of the stock market during the life of a proposed option. Individual stock prices can be expected to be influenced to some degree by the general level of the market.

Rarely do all the factors considered in evaluating risk point definitely to a very high or a very low risk. In practice, stocks will tend toward one or the other extreme. A composite of a low-risk situation would be a stock with a low price-earnings ratio, steadily rising earnings, low volatility with the stock price near the low end of the high-low range for the year, and a large number of common shares outstanding. The high-risk situation would be characterized by a stock with a high price-earnings ratio, sharply fluctuating earnings, a high ratio of high to low prices for the year, with the stock price near the year's high, and a thin market for its shares.

Some generalizations can be made about the types of option-writing opportunities which yield the highest percent return per year and, of course, involve the greatest risks.

1. Percentage price movements of low-priced stocks are often substantial, and these stocks are often attractive speculative vehicles for option buyers. The volatility of such stocks may increase the risk for option writers, but generally, the lower the stock price the higher the annual percent return on investment.

2. The premiums offered for Straddles, Calls and Puts at a given strike price are in the approximate respective ratio of 10:6:4. The same ratio reflects the generally accepted risk levels of each type of transaction, and the usual annual returns on investment (when the cash reserves which may be necessary for the Puts are taken into account).

3. Stocks that rapidly fluctuate in price on heavy volume command larger premiums at a given strike price.

4. Stocks enjoying publicity concerning a pending merger or acquisition, a new product development, or unusual or unexpected earnings, often, if only briefly, arouse investor interest. During the period of interest unusually attractive premiums are offered. Option writers are often surprised at how options on a stock currently attracting conventional investors can command attractive premiums while with a waning of investor interest the options on the same stock at the same strike price will find no buyers even at considerably lower premiums.

5. Secondary issues tend to be more volatile than "blue-chip" stocks and usually command higher premiums.

6. Shorter term options usually offer a higher percent return per year on investment. But a superficial analysis can be seriously misleading, and the option writer should analyze each situation individually.

Despite the most careful analysis of the risks involved, some of the option writer's transactions will inevitably not work out as he had hoped. Consider these three cases where the market price has unexpectedly fallen below the strike price at expiration of the option. The option writer may be left holding stock purchased as security for a Call. He may have sold a Put expecting the market price to rise and the Put to expire unexercised, and will find himself put the stock. He may have sold a Straddle expecting the Call to be exercised, and instead be put the stock. In the last two cases, if he is still confident in the stock, the option writer can use his cash reserves to purchase it and hold it. In this situation his loss is only on paper and is not realized until he sells the stock that he has been put at a loss. Patient holding may see the stock recover to the strike price and beyond. But if the option writer does not have a sufficient cash reserve, he will have to sell the stock at what he might consider a depressed price and take an irrevocable loss.

The amount of cash held in reserve relative to the number of Puts and Straddles sold will vary with different programs. The high-risk option-writing program will maintain small cash reserves relative to the number of Puts and Straddles sold. In this case the option writer relies heavily on the validity of his risk appraisal and is taking the risk that if the stock is put to him he may be forced to sell it immediately at a considerable disadvantage, unable to hold it because he lacks cash reserves. He accepts this risk because he prefers to use his available cash to write more options and thereby increase his potential annual return on investment rather than to maintain cash reserves. The low-

Risks in Selling Stock Options

risk option-writing program will maintain a large cash reserve relative to the Puts and Straddles sold. The option writer is allowing for a larger margin of error in his original appraisal of the risks in selling the options. He is prepared to purchase and hold stocks put to him and not be forced to sell them at what may be depressed prices. When he sells the stock, he wishes to choose the time and the price of the sale.

The cash reserves may be in the form of cash in excess of margin requirements held in the option writer's account. Option writers may also choose to keep the equivalent of a reserve in stock that they expect will remain stable in price and perhaps even appreciate. Options will, of course, not be written on such stock, but some risk is involved. The reserve stock may have to be sold to generate the cash necessary for purchase of any stock put. The sale could be disadvantageous and losses may be sustained because of a decline in the price of the stock.

Here is a summary of the characteristics of high-risk and low-risk option-writing programs:

High-Risk Option-Writing Programs

1. Low cash reserves relative to the number of Puts and Straddles written.

2. High proportion of Straddles relative to Puts and Calls written.

3. High proportion of stocks in the option writer's portfolio on option.

4. Options written on secondary and volatile stocks.

5. Options written primarily on low-priced stocks.

6. Call and Straddle options written without stock as security—naked options.

Low-Risk Option-Writing Programs

1. Sufficient cash reserves to purchase stock which may be put on all Straddle and Put options written.

2. High proportion of Calls and Puts relative to Straddles written.

3. Moderate proportion of stocks from the option writer's portfolio on option.

4. Options written on stocks with a history of relative price stability and higher investment stature.

5. Options written primarily on intermediate-priced stocks.

6. Call and Straddle options written only with stock held as security—no naked options.

Many investors are attracted to option writing because most of the transactions lend themselves to objective, unemotional analysis. Once the sale is made, the option writer's course of action is fixed until the contract expires. Moreover, he can be reasonably confident of a profit, and he is not as subject to the psychological and emotional stresses of the conventional investor who watches his fortune rise and fall with the stock price. The option writer who sells naked options, however, is much more subject to such stresses. Some people can tolerate high levels of stress and still maintain their capacity to make investment decisions objectively. However, even some very experienced option writers are often psychologically affected by the dangers of rising prices in the stocks on which they have sold naked options. And they will often buy stocks at high prices to cover these options and eliminate the emotional burden of a large potential loss, even after committing themselves to the risky option sale on what they thought was a sound basis. The sale of naked options should be engaged in only sparingly even in the high-risk programs.

High-risk option-writing programs characterized by low reserves can be seriously jeopardized by severe market declines such as the ones which occurred in 1962 and to a lesser extent in 1966. In these cases the option writer may find himself put almost all the Straddles and Puts he has written. His cash reserves are quickly depleted and he is faced with selling the stock put to him immediately in the market for irrevocable losses. Moreover, in the case of Straddles and Calls, whatever stock he held for security has also declined in value.

All option writers should continuously reappraise the general near-term trend of the market. If stock prices seem likely to decline, the option writer with a high-risk program will begin to include a higher proportion of individual Calls and Puts, larger cash reserves, and Straddles written on higher grade stocks. Conversely, if the market seems likely to rise, there should be changes in a low-risk program. A higher proportion of Straddles relative to individual Calls and Puts may be written, cash reserves reduced, and options may be written on secondary issues with higher yields on investment.

Some stocks seem to be particularly attractive option-writing vehicles, much in demand by option buyers, and commanding attractive premiums. These stocks may not necessarily be in favor with the conventional investor looking for rapid price appreciation. Continuous study of such stocks enables an option writer to get a "feel" for them and, over months or even years, to write many profitable options on them. This "feel" may enable the option writer to take advantage of normal price fluctuations, purchasing at attractive prices and, perhaps, selling options at higher prices. The option writer may be enjoying handsome percent returns on his investments by selling options on these stocks even though over a substantial period of time the stock price moves in a sidewise price channel. In fact, an option writer often loses interest in one of his favorite stocks when conventional investors begin to favor it and the market price advances sharply. To write options on such stock at higher prices may result in a lower annual percent return on investment and a substantially higher level of risk. Another advantage of concentrating on a limited number of stocks is that the option broker will remember them and channel inquiries for attractive option sales quickly and directly to the option writer.

Diversification is a virtue in a conventional investment program and also in an option-writing program. However, in no event should "spreading the risk" be used to justify writing an option with less than the proper amount of analysis and evaluation of the stock. Two factors limit the amount of diversification consistent with a properly executed option-writing program: money and time. Each stock on which one or more options are written will require an investment of perhaps one to several thousand dollars. The amount of capital available will limit the number of stocks in an option-writing program. Every stock in the program deserves constant study and analysis before and during the term of the option. The time available for such study will limit the number of stocks that can be handled by the option writer.

VIII

Evaluation
of Option Bids

Option writers develop the ability to recognize attractive option bids through long experience. Perhaps dozens of bids have been presented on a particular stock at various times. The latest bid may look good to the option writer only if the premium and the resulting percent return on investment is comparable to the best offers he has heard. In a negotiation with the option buyer through the option broker he can state that higher bids have been offered before on this or similar stocks, and that he will accept no smaller premium. Of course, the circumstances may have since changed, and option buyers may not be willing to pay as much as previously for a particular option. Nevertheless, knowing the previous bids on various stocks at various strike prices is a powerful tool for negotiation. Indeed, the evaluation of many bids on many stocks will enable an option writer to recognize a potentially excellent bid on a

Evaluation of Option Bids

stock which he has not studied, subject, of course, to the risk appraisal that he will then make.

The option writer lacking experience is at a disadvantage in evaluating option bids. Accepting bids as they come along will inevitably result in good, bad and mediocre transactions. Aggressively and indiscriminately re-negotiating all bids to increase premiums will often result in good bids being lost and perhaps bids being accepted which even at the higher premiums are poor or mediocre. It must be remembered that differences of as little as $25 or $50 in a premium of several hundred dollars can result in substantial increases in percent return on investment, and make the difference between a good and mediocre or even a poor transaction. Such relatively small amounts on many options written throughout the year can substantially affect the total profits at the end of the year.

To compensate for the reader's possible lack of experience, the author has prepared a series of graphs at the end of this chapter which even novice option writers can use to recognize favorable option bids. The family of curves in these graphs rank the annual percent return of a proposed option bid against the returns from many other actual option bids at the same strike price. The curves were prepared from data supplied by a leading option broker for several hundred options written during 1967. The broker supplied the strike price, the premium accepted by the option writer, and the type and duration of the option. Using the graphs at the end of Chapter VI, the annual percent return on investment was obtained for each option and the results plotted on the graphs at the end of this chapter. Then a family of three curves was determined from the points. The middle or "50 percentile" curve indicates that the annual percent return on investment for 50% of the options sampled was above this line, and 50% below. Bids that fall below the 25 percentile curve or above the 75 percentile curve are, respectively, within the bottom and top quarter of the options sampled with respect to annual percent return on investment. *Also noted on the curves are the premiums equivalent to the percent annual return on investment.* The premiums, of course, do not change when the margin requirements change.

The percentile ranking curves reflect the annual percent return for premiums based on an 80% margin requirement. A change in margin requirements changes the annual percent return for a given premium and strike price. The graphs in Chapter VI will be redrawn according to the new margin requirements, in the manner previously indicated. The percentile ranking curves can also be adjusted as follows: Take the premiums marked on the percentile ranking curves and determine the annual percent return for each one of them on the revised graphs in Chapter VI. Then plot the annual percent returns at the various strike prices to arrive at a revised family of percentile ranking curves.

The graphs presented here can be used to help evaluate the attractiveness of a particular option bid. Again, the graphs involve only 95-day and six month and 10 day Put, Call and Straddle options. When an option bid is presented, the percent return on investment per year as reflected in the premium can be determined by the graphs in Chapter VI. The percentile rating is determined by plotting the point at which the strike price of the bid and the annual percent return on investment intersect. The relative vertical position of the point with respect to the percentile curves will determine the percentile rating. Obviously, the higher the percentile rating the more favorable the bid. The risk appraisal must also be considered, however. An excellent bid would be one in which the risk was low or moderate and the percentile ranking of the bid was above the 75 percentile or in the upper quarter of all bids offered at the particular price. A poor bid would be one in which the risk was moderate or substantial and the bid was below the 25 percentile curve.

The percentile ranking curves are based on options written in 1967. How valid will they be in future years? During the past few years, premiums have remained relatively stable with perhaps a slight tendency to rise. It must be remembered that in a given year, the level of premiums offered can vary somewhat with the course of the stock market. Active, rising markets bring higher premiums and more option bids; falling markets are reflected in lower premiums and fewer option bids. But it is most unlikely that the general configurations of the percentile curves given in the graphs will change. It is also unlikely that the relative difference between the curves for the various options will change significantly. Here are some of the most significant facts reflected in the curves:

1. The lowest-priced stocks bring the highest return on investment for all options. The return on stocks costing $40 and more appears to be almost independent of the strike price.

2. Higher returns on low-priced stocks are more pronounced in six month and 10 day options than in 95-day options.

3. Ninety-five-day options yield consistently higher returns than six month and 10 day options. But the lower the strike price, the less the advantage. At strike prices above $40, the return on the shorter option is approximately 50% greater, while at strike prices as low as $10 the return is only 25% greater.

4. Straddles consistently yield higher returns than Calls by a ratio approximately reflecting the normal differences in premiums at a given strike price.

5. The differences in percent return on investment for 95-day and six month and 10 day Puts is slight for low-priced stocks, and it increases only moderately for 95-day Puts at higher prices.

To summarize, here are the steps to be taken by the option writer in evaluating a particular bid. The option broker refers the bid to the writer stating premium, type of option, and strike price. The writer obtains the percent return on investment from the graphs in Chapter VI. He appraises the risk by considering the factors discussed in Chapter VII. If the risk level is tolerable, he uses the percentile ranking curves to compare the present bid with the many similar bids at the same strike price from which the curves were derived. If the risk is considered moderate or substantial, the bid must be above the 75 percentile curve to be attractive. If the risk is low, the option writer may consider a bid near the 50 percentile curve. But knowing that many similar bids have been written at higher premiums, the option writer may also be encouraged to renegotiate for a higher premium. No matter what the level of risk, bids ranking below the 25 percentile curve may be totally unacceptable to the option writer without a serious attempt to negotiate for a higher price.

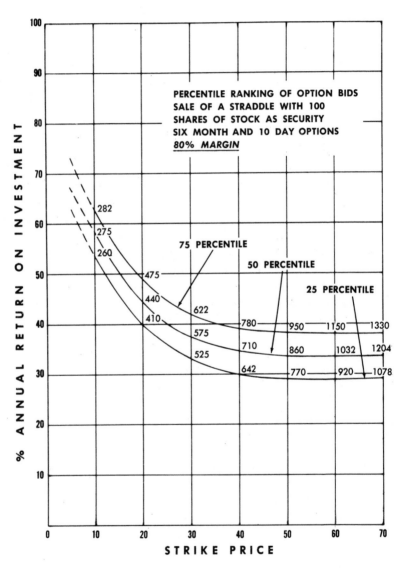

PERCENTILE RANKING OF OPTION BIDS
SALE OF A STRADDLE WITH 100
SHARES OF STOCK AS SECURITY
SIX MONTH AND 10 DAY OPTIONS
80% MARGIN

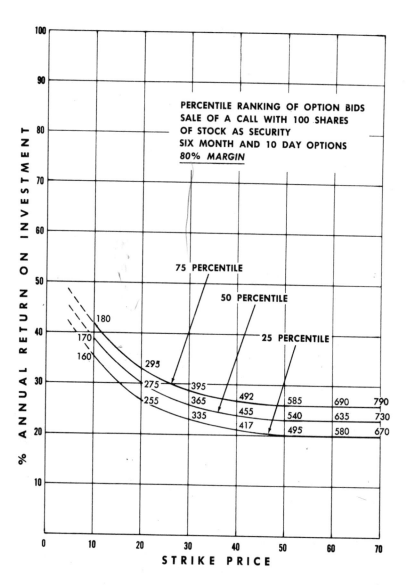

Evaluation of Option Bids

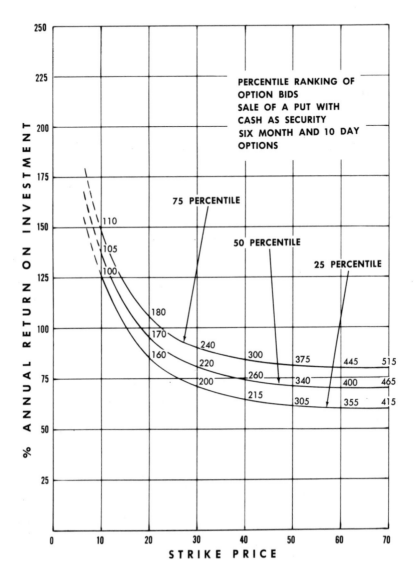

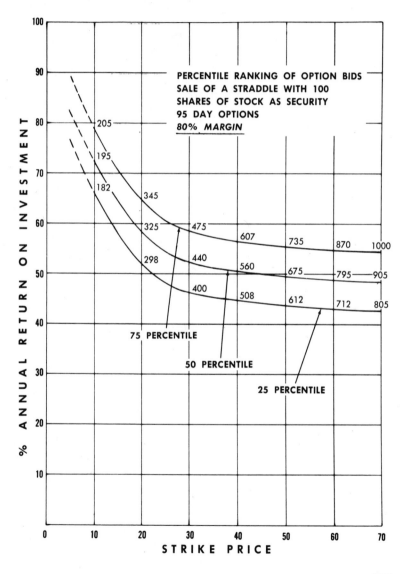

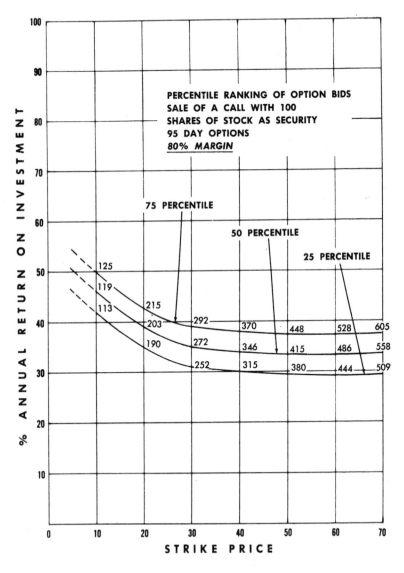

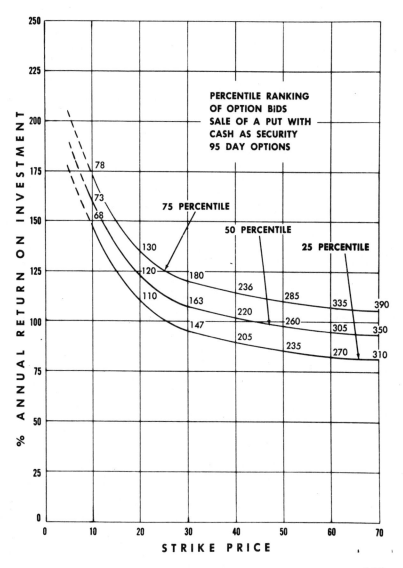

IX

Margin Considerations

The basic margin rules involved in the sale of individual options have already been discussed in Chapter VI. In an option-writing account, the cash required by margin rules for security of the options written changes with the market prices of the stocks involved. Favorable market changes will result in a reduction in the cash requirements and "release money" available for further investment. This release money is the additional sum that can be currently borrowed from the broker under margin rules. Adverse price changes, on the other hand, will result in increased cash requirements for security. However, brokers may allow considerable latitude before demanding additional cash for security over and above that required to write the options initially. When the cash security falls below minimum margin requirements, restrictions, as outlined below, are placed on the account. Option writers must allow for these restrictions and not permit them to seriously hamper their investment programs.

When an option is written, cash is required for the purchase of stock and/or the required cash security. The premium received by the option writer is also entered in the account immediately as part of the cash requirement. Any cash in the account over and above that required as minimum security for all options still in force can be used as part of the security for the new option sale. Even if the overall account shows a debit for minimum cash security, options can be written provided the minimum cash security is put up for those particular sales. The cash balance of the account is calculated by the option broker's margin clerk on the day each new option is written. For that purpose he uses the previous day's closing prices for all stocks in the account.

Calculating the margin status of an account can be tedious especially in a large, active, complex program, and many option writers prefer to leave the job to the margin clerk. The option broker will arrange that such calculations be made as frequently as possible, but it can take from a few minutes to an hour of the margin clerk's time depending on the complexity of the account. Computers are generally not yet being used to make these calculations. It is impossible to alert the option writer every time he has excess cash or "release money," sometimes called "additional borrowing power," in his account, yet attractive option sales opportunities may appear at any time. Unless the option writer can at least estimate the status of his own account he may miss such opportunities, not realizing he has release money which he may borrow from the broker and use for investment. A call to the margin clerk to make the calculation will get him the result, but it may be too late to take advantage of the opportunity. Whether or not an option writer decides to continuously monitor the margin status of his account, he should at least be familiar with the necessary rules and techniques.

The example below illustrates the principles of margin calculations in an option writer's account. The options are listed in tabular form along with the strike and market prices used to calculate the original cash security and the current cash security required at the time the calculation is made. While in practice exact prices should be used, fractions in the strike and market prices have been omitted here. It is further assumed that market and strike prices were identical when the options were written.

In accordance with the basic margin rules for Puts, Calls and Straddles, release money becomes available when the market price is above the strike price for Puts, and for the Put portion of Straddles with stock as security. Additional cash security is required in this case for naked Calls and the Call portion of naked Straddles. With market price below strike price, money is released for naked Calls and additional cash security is required for Puts, and the Put portions of Straddles both naked and with stock as security. The maximum release money will be equal to the original cash security required at the time the option was written. A Call with 100 shares of stock as security requires no additional cash security no matter what the price of the stock.

Referring to the hypothetical account shown in the table at the end of this chapter, the current margin status is to be determined. First, the current cash security required for each option is calculated according to the margin rules. In this example, the total is $5,575.

Next, the marginable value of stocks held as security for options is tabulated at the market or strike price, whichever is lower. The total is $10,400. Even if the market price is

Margin Considerations

higher than the strike price, the stock is valued only at the strike price, for that is the price at which it will be called. Conversely, if the market price is lower than the strike price, the stock will not be called, and is worth only the market price.

Having calculated the total cash security requirement and the value of the stock used as security, the value of all other stock in the account is calculated at current market prices. The previous month's broker's statement of the margin account will show a cash credit or cash debit which is also used in the margin calculation. The account should, of course, be brought up-to-date if transactions have taken place after the statement was prepared by the broker. For purposes of calculation in the example below it is assumed that $29,600 is the market value of all stock in the account other than the stock used as security for the options. There is a cash debit of $1,000 in the account which is money borrowed from the broker.

The format for calculation of the margin status of the account used in the example at the end of the chapter is presented below.

Stock as security	10,400
All other stock	29,600
Total	40,000
Maximum allowable borrowing (20%) on stock	
at 80% margin requirement	8,000
Cash security required	5,575
Maximum allowable borrowing	2,425
Cash already borrowed from broker	1,000
Total release money	1,425

The $1,425 is additional money that can be borrowed from the broker. It can be used as cash for the purchase of stock, as cash security for writing more options, or it can be taken out of the account completely.

In the preceding example, the account is "above 80% margin." That is to say, there is $1,425 in cash in the account over and above the minimum required by margin rules. Suppose the "cash borrowed from broker" had been $4,000 instead of $1,000. Since the maximum allowable borrowing from the broker is $2,425 according to the 80% margin requirement, the account is "below 80% margin" by $1,575. In this situation, the following restrictions are placed on the account:

1. Cash cannot be taken out of the account.

2. When stock is sold, only 30% of the proceeds can be taken out of the account in cash. And it can only be taken out of the account on the day of sale. The remainder is applied to the cash deficit required to bring the account up to the minimum 80% margin requirement.

3. If stock is sold and the 30% allowable cash is not taken out of the account, it too is applied to the cash deficit required to bring the account to the minimum 80% margin requirement.

When the option writer needs cash from his account the disadvantages of being "below 80% margin" are considerable. If he sells stock he can only take out 30% of the proceeds. Had the account been "above 80% margin," he could have taken out 80% of the proceeds from the same sale.

If stock is sold in an option-writing account "below 80% margin," and no cash is taken out, all the proceeds are applied to the cash deficit. The problem here is that stock previously available for investment or as security for new option sales is converted to cash, and the cash is frozen in the account. There is, however, one very important and advantageous exception to this rule currently in effect (1968). In an account "below 80% margin" when stock is sold, an equivalent amount of another stock can be purchased with the proceeds if purchased on the same day as

Margin Considerations

the original stock is sold. The option writer can thus maintain his position in stocks to be used for investment or as security for new option writing. Of course, timing may be a problem. He may not find an attractive stock to buy on the day he sells.

The restrictions placed on accounts "below 80% margin" make many option writers maintain cash reserves in their account to avoid the situation. Nevertheless, severe general market declines may even cause accounts with substantial reserves to fall "below 80% margin." To avoid any possibility of such a situation occurring may require very large cash reserves which are not earning profits under normal conditions. Even low-risk accounts should maintain sufficient reserves to take care of moderate fluctuations in market prices, and accept the chance that occasionally their accounts will be "below 80% margin."

Option writers engaging in high-risk investment programs usually maintain their accounts only slightly "above 80% margin." Release money generated by reduced cash security requirements is continuously borrowed from the broker and re-invested in stock for investment or as security for new option sales. But because even minor adverse market price changes will cause the account to go "below 80% margin," the high-risk account is maintained under the restrictions discussed above a substantial part of the time.

When an option expires or is exercised, the cash security for it is immediately released in the option writer's account. This cash can be borrowed from the broker and used for any purpose, as will be seen from the examples below. For the hypothetical account, assume that the market price is as shown in the table on the day that the option expires. Remember that if the account is "below 80% margin," the release money cannot be removed from the account. This cash will be applied to the margin deficit unless it is used to buy an equivalent amount of stock on the day it is released.

Stock B—The Call expires unexercised. The option writer may now borrow an additional $100—the release money—from the broker for any use he may wish to make of it.

Stock C—The Call is exercised. The option writer will buy stock to deliver, taking a $500 loss. The rest of the release money, $1,050, is now available to the option writer, if he wishes to borrow it.

Stock D—The Put is exercised at $20, and the option writer decides to keep the stock. To pay for it, margin rules allow him to borrow 20% of the market value—$340—and borrow an additional $725, the release money. He must still supply an additional $935 in cash.

Stock E—The Put expires unexercised, making the $400 release money available to be borrowed from the broker if the option writer desires.

Stock G—The Put is exercised at $20 and the option writer decides to sell this stock in the market, taking a $300 loss. The rest of the release money, $425, can now be borrowed from the broker.

Stock H—The Call is exercised and the option writer decides to deliver the stock that was used as security. In addition to the proceeds of the stock sale, he can now borrow $250, the release money, and perhaps purchase $2,800 worth of new stock.

MARGIN CALCULATION OF OPTION WRITER'S ACCOUNT

STOCK	SHARES HELD	OPTION SOLD	STRIKE PRICE (1)	CURRENT MARKET PRICE	CASH SECURITY NEEDED (2)		MARGINABLE STOCK VALUE (3)	
					ORIGINAL	CURRENT	ORIGINAL	CURRENT
A	100	Call	20	17	0	0	2000	1700
B	0	Call	25	20	750	100	—	—
C	0	Call	30	35	900	1550	—	—
D	0	Put	20	17	500	725	—	—
E	0	Put	25	28	625	400	—	—
F	0	Put	30	40	750	0	—	—
G	100	Straddle	20	17	500	725	2000	1700
H	100	Straddle	25	30	625	250	2500	2500
I	100	Straddle	30	40	750	0	3000	3000
J	0	Straddle	20	17	600	725	—	—
K	50	Straddle	30	40	750	1100	1500	1500
					$6750	$5575	$11000	$10400

NOTES:

(1) Strike price was the market price at the time the option was written.
(2) Calculated according to the margin rules explained in Chapter VI.
(3) Total value of stock held as security at market or strike price, whichever is lower.

X

Tax Considerations

Option writers as well as conventional investors try to minimize their tax liabilities on profits. Knowledge of the current tax laws for the conventional purchase and sale of securities is essential for the option writer. He must also know the special tax laws which apply to option writing. Option brokers and professional tax advisors can supply official literature on all aspects of pertinent tax laws. This chapter summarizes the basic tax laws applying to option writers.

Authorities familiar with the option-writing tax laws have confirmed the essential validity of the interpretations in this chapter. The laws are, of course, those in effect at present (1968). No attempt has been made to cover the tax laws applicable to conventional investment programs or those dealing with capital losses and the methods of shifting income or loss from one year to another.

1. Short-term capital gains and losses result from the sale of capital assets (i.e. securities) held for six months

or less. These gains are taxed as though they were ordinary income.

2. Long-term capital gains and losses result from the sale of capital assets (i.e. securities) held for more than six months. They are taxed at one-half of the applicable ordinary income tax rate but never more than 25%.

3. When a Call is exercised and the *option writer* sells a security as a result, his net sale price is the income realized from the sale plus his premium and minus brokerage fees, expenses and taxes. Whether it is a long or short-term transaction depends on the length of time the option writer has held the specific lot of stock delivered for sale upon exercise of the Call. When a Call is exercised, the *option buyer's* cost is the purchase price of the stock, plus brokerage fees, taxes, expenses and the premium he paid for the Call. To determine the long or short-term status of the stock, the buyer's holding period begins when the Call is exercised and does *not* include the length of time the Call was in effect.

4. When a Put is exercised and the *option writer* buys a security as a result, his purchase price is the amount he paid for the stock plus brokerage fees and other expenses and minus the premium he received for the Put. To determine the long or short-term status of the stock, the option writer's holding period begins with the date the Put is exercised and does *not* include the time the Put was in effect. When a Put is exercised, the *option buyer's* sale price includes brokerage fees and other expenses minus the premium he has paid for the Put. The acquisition of a Put by an option buyer is considered equivalent to a short sale. The exercise of the Put is the closing of the short sale for tax purposes and special rules apply. In general, profits resulting from the exercise of Puts, except in certain special

circumstances, are short-term. Option buyers should investigate the rather complex rules that apply in such a situation.

5. Put and Call contracts are capital assets, except for dealers in options. Profits or losses resulting from the sale of option contracts by option buyers are either long or short-term for tax purposes depending on the holding period of the options.

6. When either side of a Straddle is exercised, the option writer must divide the premium received. The Internal Revenue Service has ruled that an arbitrary allocation of 55% of the premium to the Call and 45% to the Put will be permitted.

7. The portion of the premium allocated to the expired unexercised Put or Call portion of a Straddle, when one side of the Straddle has been exercised, is treated as a short-term gain regardless of the duration of the Straddle. Such short-term gains can be used to offset short-term losses.

8. The premiums on expired and unexercised individual options, with the exception of the rules applying to Straddles set forth in 7, are treated as ordinary income and are accounted for on tax returns under the heading "other income." Such income cannot be used to offset short-term losses.

9. If an investor sells part of his holding of a given stock, the stock that he bought first will be delivered unless he instructs his broker at the time of sale to deliver stock bought later.

10. When securities are sold at a loss, the loss will not be recognized for tax purposes if within thirty days either before or after the sale, the same securities or an option on those securities has been acquired. This is often called the "wash sale" rule.

To illustrate the application of the above rules by option

Tax Considerations

writers, some typical transactions are described below. For simplicity, brokerage fees, expenses and dividends that might reduce the strike prices have been omitted.

CASE I—A 95-day Straddle is sold on ABC stock for a premium of $200 at a strike price of $10. The option writer simultaneously purchases 100 shares of ABC stock as security at $10. One month later the market price advances to $15, and a six month and 10 day Call is sold for a premium of $150 with the simultaneous purchase of another lot of 100 shares of ABC stock as security at $15. Upon expiration of the Straddle, the Call portion of the Straddle is exercised. The Put portion of the Straddle expires unexercised, and 45% of the Straddle premium, or $90, is treated as a short-term gain. The sale price realized on the stock is $1,000, plus 55% of the Straddle premium, or $110, resulting in a price per share of $11.10. The option writer authorizes his broker in writing to deliver the stock purchased at $15 two months previously as security for the Call, and takes a short-term loss of $390 ($15 less $11.10 for each share). Three months later the Call is exercised at a sale price of $1,500, plus the $150 premium or $16.50 per share. The stock delivered for sale is the lot purchased more than six months previously at $10, resulting in a long-term gain of $650.

A summary of the results of the above transactions is as follows: a $650 long-term gain, a $90 short-term gain, and a $390 short-term loss. The $390 short-term loss is used to offset the $90 short-term gain and other short-term gains which may have resulted from expired unexercised portions of Straddle options, normal short-term trading profits, and profits from exercised 95-day Call and Straddle options.

CASE II—A six month and 10 day Straddle is sold on ABC stock at a strike price of $20 for a premium of $400. Simultaneously, 100 shares of stock are bought as security at $20.

Forty-five days before expiration of the option, another 100 shares are purchased at a market price of $30 per share. The Call portion of the Straddle is exercised by the option buyer six months and one day after purchase of the option, just long enough to qualify for a long-term gain. The option writer authorizes his broker in writing to deliver the stock purchased at $30. A short-term loss of $780 is realized ($3,000 purchase price less $2,220 sale price). The premium on the expired unexercised Put portion of the Straddle is 45% of $400 or $180 and qualifies as a short-term gain. Thirty-one days after the exercise of the Call the original shares purchased at $20 were sold at the then market price of $32 for a long-term profit of $1,200.

In the above case, the "wash sale" (30-day) rule was honored. The tax loss was established because no stock was bought within thirty days before or after the option sale. The option writer, of course, risked some of his profit by purchasing stock at a high price more than a month before expiration of the option, delivering that stock upon exercise of the option, and then waiting another month to sell the original stock.

CASE III—A six month and 10 day Put is sold on ABC stock at a strike price of $20 and a premium of $200. With a market price of $19 at expiration, the Put is exercised. The option writer's net purchase price is $2,000, less the $200 premium, or $18 per share. On the day of purchase, a 95-day Straddle is sold for a premium of $300 and a strike price of $19. The Call portion of the Straddle is subsequently exercised and the Put expires. The sale price of the stock is $1,900 plus 55% of $300 or $2,065. The result is a short-term profit of $265 ($2,065 less $1,800). The Put portion of the Straddle premium is 45% of $300 or $135. All profits are short-term.

In the above case, although a six month and 10 day Put

Tax Considerations

was exercised, the holding period for the purchased stock began only the day it was purchased.

CASE IV—A 95-day Straddle is sold on ABC stock for a $300 premium at a strike price of $20 with a simultaneous purchase of 100 shares of ABC stock as security at $20 per share. Both the Put and Call portions of the Straddle expired unexercised with the market price at $20 a share at expiration. The $300 premium is reported as option income under the "other income" heading in the tax return. A 95-day Call is then sold at a strike price of $20 and a premium of $175. With the market price of $19 per share at expiration, the Call expires unexercised. The $175 premium for the Call is also considered ordinary income. At a strike price of $19 a six month and 10 day Put is sold for a $200 premium. One day later a six month and 10 day Call is sold at the same strike price of $19 and a premium of $250. The Put expires unexercised and the $200 premium is considered "other income" on the tax return. The Call is exercised the next day at a sale price of $1,900 plus the $250 premium for a total of $2,150 less the $2,000 originally paid for the stock, resulting in a long-term capital gain of $150.

In the above Case, the expired Put is not considered part of a Straddle even though a Call was sold the next day at the same strike price. A Straddle is defined as the simultaneous sale of a Put and a Call at the same strike price for the same period of time. Had the expired Put been part of a Straddle, the premium would have been a short-term gain and could be balanced against short-term losses. "Other income," which is considered ordinary income for tax purposes, cannot be offset by short-term losses.

CASE V—An option buyer purchases a six month and 10 day Call on ABC stock at a strike price of $20 and a premium of $400. Six months and one day after purchase, the market price of the stock is $30 per share. The option buyer asks his broker to purchase the Call for $1,000. The Call is a capital asset that cost $400. Selling it to the broker for $1,000 results in a long-term capital gain of $600 for the option buyer since the holding period is greater than six months. The Call is worth $1,000 to the broker because it enables him to purchase stock at $20 per share from the option writer and sell it in the market at $30 per share.

Had the option buyer exercised his option at $20 per share and sold the stock in the market immediately at $30 per share, he would have realized a $600 profit on the overall transaction, but it would have been a short-term capital gain. The holding period for the stock sold began only the day the stock was purchased upon exercise of the Call.

CASE VI—An option buyer purchases a six month and 10 day Put on ABC stock for a premium of $300 and a strike price of $20. One day before the sixth month anniversary of the purchase of the Put, the market price of the stock is $25 a share. With only eleven days remaining before the option expires, the option buyer sees little chance of profitably exercising his Put. So he asks his broker to purchase the essentially worthless Put for $1, and he takes a $299 short-term loss to apply against his short-term gains. A worthless Call can also be sold in the same fashion to establish short-term losses.

CASE VII—A six month and 10 day Straddle is sold on ABC stock at a strike price of $10 for a premium of $300 with simultaneous purchase of 100 shares of stock as security. At expiration the stock has advanced to $20, and the Call portion of the Straddle is exercised. The Put portion expires unexercised and the $135 equivalent to 45% of the premium is a short-term gain. If the stock held as security is delivered to the option buyer a $165 long-term gain results. The option writer, however, chooses to purchase stock in the market at $20 on the day the option is exercised and

Tax Considerations

he instructs his broker to deliver this lot to the option buyer. In this case he takes a short-term loss of $835. The $835 is the difference between the purchase price of $2,000 and the sale price of $10 per share plus the premium for the Call portion of the Straddle. The original shares held as security for the option can now be used to secure the sale of other options or they can be sold in the market. The 30-day "wash sale" rule, however, restricts the sale of the stock within thirty days after the establishment of the short-term tax loss. Option writers widely use the technique discussed in this case to establish short-term tax losses. The 30-day "wash sale" rule states that a security cannot be purchased thirty days before or after a sale of the same, or a substantially similar security to establish a short-term tax loss. To establish a tax loss the investor must either purchase the same security at least thirty-one days before the intended sale to establish the short-term loss, or wait thirty-one days after the sale to purchase the same stock to reestablish his position. If he purchases the stock thirty-one days before the sale, he accepts the burden of "doubling up" on his securities. If he waits thirty-one days after the sale, he assumes the risk that the stock price will rise. He will then have to pay more for the stock to reestablish his position than he received for the stock that he sold to establish his short-term loss. This interpretation of the 30-day "wash sale" rule allows the option writer to purchase stock for the purpose of establishing a tax loss on the day the option buyer exercises his option. The stock is bought not to maintain a position in the security but to deliver to honor the obligation represented by the option contract. On the other hand, the option writer cannot simultaneously sell the stock held as security for the option, because this would establish a short-term loss compensated for by a long-term gain. The option writer must assume the risk of waiting thirty-one days after establishing the short-term loss before selling the stock held as security for the option. The long-term gain thus achieved would depend on the market price of the stock at time of sale. Of course, the risk of waiting thirty-one days after establishing the short sale can be eliminated by "doubling up" or purchasing the stock at least thirty-one days before exercise of the option and delivering this lot of stock.

A properly executed option-writing program will result in an accumulation of substantial short-term gains from the expiration of unexercised Put and Call components of Straddle options. The exercise of 95- and 65-day Call options and the Call components of Straddle options, as well as conventional short-term trading, will result in more short-term gains. As has been illustrated, there are techniques which can be used to develop short-term losses and compensate for them with long-term profits. To develop situations where these techniques work most effectively, option writers often select volatile stocks and sell several Call and Straddle options on them at successively higher prices at various times. Upon exercise of the Calls and Call components of Straddles written at lower prices, stock purchased as security for higher-priced options written less than six months previously, are delivered and result in short-term losses. The stock purchased at the lower prices then becomes security for the options written at higher strike prices. Upon exercise of the options at the higher strike prices, attractive long-term capital gains are achieved. The 30-day "wash sale" rule must, of course, be observed in these transactions.

Option writers seeking long-term gains and risking only short-term losses are also attracted to the purchase of six month and 10 day options. Successful purchases will result in long-term gains. The lost premium in unsuccessful transactions can be converted to a short-term loss by selling the option just before the six month purchase anniversary.

XI

Record Keeping

An active option-writing program will involve a large number of transactions per year relative to the amount of capital invested. Proper and timely record keeping is an absolute essential so that income tax liabilities can be accurately determined. In a complex program, records should be completed monthly. Proper record keeping will also enable the option writer to take full advantage of the tax laws. It has been demonstrated, for example, that Calls or Straddles upon exercise may require the option writer to deliver one "round lot" of stock out of perhaps many that he holds. His selection will be based on his ability to quickly determine the purchase date and price of each lot of stock in his account.

The option broker will send certain records to the option writer which will form the basis of his record keeping system. All these records must be kept permanently in a file for the year's transactions for possible inspection by the tax authorities, as well as for future reference. These records are:

1. *Transaction Confirmation*—When a purchase or sale is executed, a confirmation is immediately sent with the following information:

> a. Name of security and number of shares, or description of option sold or purchased.
> b. Trade date and settlement date.
> c. Price per share.
> d. Gross amount of money involved in purchase or sale.
> e. Commission and taxes.
> f. Net amount.

2. *Option Exercise or Expiration Confirmation*—Immediate notice is sent terminating an outstanding option either through exercise or expiration.

3. *Dividends Deposited*—Immediate notice is sent of all applicable dividends credited.

4. *Monthly Statement*—A monthly summary of all transactions executed and the current status of the account is sent with the following information:

> a. Cash credit or debit in the account, including the balance forward and the closing balance.
> b. All transactions involving purchase and sale of securities and options including trade and/or settlement date and number of shares.
> c. Cash deposits and withdrawals.
> d. Dividends credited.
> e. Interest charged for margin money borrowed.
> f. Number of shares of all stocks in the account.

124

g. List of outstanding options with their expiration dates and strike prices.

When the option writer receives the Transaction Confirmation, he should summarize all pertinent information on his Transaction Summary Sheet. Two such Sheets should be maintained for each year, one for stocks and options sold, and one for stocks and options purchased. Examples are included at the end of this chapter with actual transactions recorded.

Here are the transactions recorded in the sample Transaction Summary Sheets:

Transaction Summary Sheet—Sales 1968

1. *Security A*—A Straddle is sold for $300. The option writer will find it necessary for tax calculations to "split" the premium received between the Put and Call components in a 45:55 ratio as discussed in the preceding chapter.

2. *Security B*—One hundred and fifty shares of stock are sold, but the sale is recorded as two separate transactions because two separate lots of stock purchased at different times are delivered to the buyer. The notes column specifies the actual lots of stock and their purchase dates. Tax considerations are again involved. One of the two lots will qualify for a long-term capital gain while the other will be sold for a short-term gain. When the stock was sold, the option writer requested his broker to specify the actual lots of stock involved in the Transaction Confirmations. Another reason for separating the transactions is that although the

two lots of stock were sold at the same time for the same market price, the sale price of the 50-share lot was reduced by the ⅛ of a point odd-lot differential.

3. *Security C*—This sale of a bond is recorded exactly the same way as a stock transaction. The bonds may have been purchased by the option writer to maintain the equivalent of a cash reserve.

4. *Security D and E*—Standard sales of Puts and Calls are recorded.

5. *Security F*—The notes indicate that this stock was purchased at a higher price and sold the same day at a lower price. This transaction is a standard technique in establishing a short-term loss. The sale could have resulted from a Call being exercised. The option writer has purchased the stock in the market and delivered that specific lot to the option buyer. The original lot of stock held as security is thus released. This transaction could also record the delivery of stock purchased on the day a naked Call was exercised.

6. *Security G*—The stock sold was held as security for a six month and 10 day Call or Straddle. It was purchased at the time of the option sale and at the strike price which was the market price. The Call was exercised three months before expiration. The option writer specified that the lot bought for security was the one to be delivered to the option buyer. He may have had several lots of that stock in his account and failure to specify the lot would have resulted in automatic delivery of the lot purchased earliest.

7. *Security H*—The notes show that the stock sold was originally purchased when a Put that he had written was exercised. For tax purposes the original purchase price of the stock must be reduced by the premium received for the Put. Thus the record must show the origin of the lot of stock as being the result of a particular Put exercised.

Transaction Summary Sheet—Purchases 1968

Security A—Standard purchases of stock are recorded. The option writer may indicate in the notes column that he has purchased stock and simultaneously sold an option, and that the stock is to serve as security for the option. Depending on the outcome of the option sale and tax considerations, he may later wish to deliver a different lot of stock if the option is exercised.

Security B—Purchase of a Call option is recorded.

Security C—The notes indicate that stock is purchased to honor a Put sold by the option writer and exercised on its expiration date.

Security D—Purchase of a Straddle option is recorded. The premium paid is "split" between the Put and Call.

Security E—Purchase of a bond is recorded.

In addition to yearly Transaction Summary Sheets, the option writer will find it advantageous to maintain a Transaction Summary Sheet for each stock in his portfolio. Maintaining a record of all transactions involving that stock will enable the option writer at a glance to determine the date of purchase and the cost of all lots of that particular stock. An active account may hold several lots of a single stock purchased over a span of years—some purchased outright and some as the result of the sale or purchase of an option. In an active option-writing program only a record of transactions for the individual stock will make it possible to deliver the most appropriate lot for maximum tax benefits to the option broker who is waiting for an answer on the other end of the telephone.

A sample Transaction Summary Sheet for an individual stock is included for study at the end of this chapter. The cost basis is the price paid less the Put premium received if the stock is purchased as the result of the exercise of a Put sold. The sales basis is the price received plus the Call premium if the stock is sold as a result of the exercise of a Call sold. To determine his sales basis, the buyer of a Put deducts the cost of the premium he paid from the price of the stock he sells when he exercises the Put. To determine his cost basis the buyer of a Call adds the cost of the premium he paid to the purchase price of the stock when he exercises the Call. The Purchase and Sale Notes column identify the options involved in the transaction. The broker's monthly statement recording all unexercised and unexpired options bought and sold should be used in conjunction with the Transaction Summary Sheet for each individual stock. An active option writer may also find it helpful to maintain a calendar on which are noted the expiration dates of the options he has written.

Transaction 1—Stock is purchased at a strike price of $10 when a Put the option writer has sold is exercised. The adjusted Cost Price is the Net Purchase Price less the $125 premium received for the Put. This lot of stock is delivered when a Call the option writer has sold is exercised twenty-one months later at a strike price of $11. The Adjusted Sales Price includes the $150 premium received for the Call.

Transaction 2—Stock is purchased at $9 per share originally as security for a six month and 10 day Call that is sold simultaneously. Although the Call is exercised at expiration, this particular lot of stock is not delivered. It is eventually sold at $20.

Transaction 3—The stock delivered upon exercise of the Call sold in Transaction 2 is purchased in the market at $14 and sold at the $9 strike price to establish a short-term loss. A 95-day Straddle is then sold at a strike price of $14 secured by the stock purchased at $9 in Transaction 2.

Transaction 4—The Put component of the Straddle sold

in Transaction 3 is exercised at a strike price of $14 with the Call component expiring unexercised. A 95-day Call is sold at a strike price of $12 and is exercised at expiration. The stock purchased ninety-five days earlier is delivered. The purchase and sale prices of the stock involved are adjusted by the premiums received for the options.

Transaction 5—In this case a Call was purchased by the option writer at a strike price of $15 and was exercised. The adjusted Cost Price is determined by adding the premium to the Net Purchase Price.

Transaction Summary Sheets are the basic records for an efficient option-writing program. In addition, there should be a supplementary file on each stock containing financial articles, quarterly surveys, annual reports, etc. Because option writers usually hold only a limited number of stocks, many of them over a span of years, it should not be difficult for them to digest, and keep for reference all pertinent information on these stocks. Many option writers also intensively follow a few stocks not in their account but which may be candidates for option-writing opportunities in the future.

Active option writers should calculate their gains and losses on all completed transactions monthly from the data recorded in the Transaction Summary Sheets. The following records should be maintained, for they are required by the Internal Revenue Service:

1. Short-term capital gains and losses.
2. Long-term capital gains and losses.
3. Short-term capital gains from expired Straddles in which one of the options has been exercised.
4. "Other income" from expired, unexercised options.

TRANSACTION SUMMARY SHEET - SALES 1968

Trade Date	Security	Number of Shares	Share Price or Strike Price	Sale Price	Commission and Other Charges	Net Sales Price	Option	Call Premium	Put Premium	Expiration Date	Notes
1/13	A	100	11⅞	–	–	300.00	STRADDLE	165.00	135.00	7/24/68	
1/16	B	100	16¾	1,675.00	27.54	1,647.46	–	–	–	–	VS. PURCHASE 1/5/67 @ 12¾
1/16	B	50	16⅝	831.25	15.21	816.04	–	–	–	–	VS. PURCHASE 9/30/67 @ 14½
1/20	C (Bonds)	1000	98 26/32	988.13	6.75	981.38	–	–	–	–	VS. PURCHASE 11/16/67
2/2	D	100	16⅛	–	–	–	PUT	–	137.50	8/12/68	
2/5	E	100	26	–	–	–	CALL	250.00	–	5/10/68	
2/9	F	100	20⅛	2,012.50	27.13	1985.37	–	–	–	–	VS. PURCHASE 2/9/68 @ 25½
2/15	G	100	8½	850.00	15.50	834.50	–	–	–	–	VS. PURCHASE 11/6/67 @ 8½ FROM CALL EXPIRING 5/16/68
2/22	H	100	30¾	3,075.00	39.80	3,035.20	–	–	–	–	VS. PURCHASE 8/24/67 @ 28 FROM PUT EXERCISED

TRANSACTION SUMMARY SHEET - PURCHASES 1968

TRADE DATE	SECURITY	NUMBER OF SHARES	SHARE PRICE OR STRIKE PRICE	PURCHASE PRICE	COMMISSION AND OTHER CHARGES	NET PURCHASE PRICE	OPTION	CALL PREMIUM	PUT PREMIUM	EXPIRATION DATE	NOTES
1/12	A	200	8⅜	1,637.50	30.38	1,667.88	—	—	—	—	SECURITY FOR (2) STRADDLES SOLD 1/12/68
1/16	B	100	20	—	—	—	CALL	350.00	—	7/26/68	
1/20	C	100	9¾	975.00	16.75	991.75	—	—	—	—	PUT EXERCISED — EXPIRES 1/20/68
1/25	D	100	15	—	—	500.00	STRADDLE	275.00	225.00	8/4/68	
1/26	E (Bonds)	1000	100½	1,005.00	6.60	1,011.60	—	—	—	—	

TRANSACTION SUMMARY SHEET - STOCK A

PURCHASE DATE	SHARE PRICE	NUMBER OF SHARES	NET PURCHASE PRICE	ADJUSTED COST BASIS OPTION PREMIUM INCLUDED	SALE DATE	SHARE PRICE	NUMBER OF SHARES	NET SALES PRICE	ADJUSTED SALES PRICE OPTION PREMIUM INCLUDED	PURCHASE NOTES	SALE NOTES
1/5/65	10	100	1017	892	9/10/66	11	100	1082	1232	PUT EXERCISED Xp[1] 1/5/65	CALL EXERCISED Xp 10/10/66
3/6/65	9	100	909	—	5/1/67	20	100	1973	—	SECURITY FOR CALL Xp 9/16/65	
9/16/65	14	100	1421	—	9/16/65	9	100	884	1034	TO ESTABLISH SHORT TERM LOSS	CALL EXERCISED Xp 9/16/65
12/21/65	14	100	1421	1286	3/26/66	12	100	1181	1331	PUT EXERCISED Xp 12/21/65	CALL EXERCISED Xp 3/26/66
8/1/67	15	100	1522	1722						PURCHASED CALL EXERCISED Xp 8/1/67	

[1] Xp = expires

XII

Analysis of Actual Option-Writing Transactions

To further illustrate the techniques of option writing, here are some examples of actual transactions from the author's own high-risk option-writing program. The margin requirement was 70% when the transactions were made, and the charts used to determine the annual percent return on investment and the percentile ranking were based on that margin requirement.

In July, 1966 the author was shown a six month and 10 day Straddle bid on Helene Curtis Industries, a well-known cosmetics company, for a premium of $425 and a strike price of $16. The charts showed an annual 64% return on investment with simultaneous purchase of stock as security. The percentile ranking curves confirmed that the bid was in the top quarter. Here then was a potentially attractive bid if the accompanying risk of a price decline was no more than moderate.

The author subscribes to one of the charting services

which plots the market price for the previous few months and provides separate charts of market prices for the past four years on most listed stocks. Quarterly and yearly earnings, cash flow, book value, and the number of common shares outstanding are included on the charts. Alternatively, the option broker could have supplied a chart and a financial profile of the company. The chart for Helene Curtis showed that during the past three months, the stock had plunged from a high of $24. In the previous year, 1965, the company had showed only a small profit, and the market price of the stock had fluctuated on historically low volume in the mid-teens. After several alternating quarterly profits and losses, the company had registered a substantial profit for the quarter ending February, 1966. The market price rose dramatically until the next quarter's report showed a small loss. At that point the stock price fell badly. Judged by the criteria outlined in Chapter VII there was a substantial risk that the market price would slip further. There was no history of stable earnings to support the price of the stock; in fact the company had at best broken even for the past three years. During the last year, the market price had fluctuated from a low of $10 to a high of $24.

The conventional investor evaluating Helene Curtis would probably conclude that prospects for price appreciation were not good until the company demonstrated stable earnings for a reasonable period of time. He would reject purchase of the stock. The option writer might agree that substantial price appreciation was unlikely in the near future. But he would see in the chart history of the stock that even though the company showed a net loss for the previous two years the stock resisted price declines below the $10 to $12 range. Further, he would note that Helene Curtis had only a little more than two million common shares outstanding, no preferred stock, and sales consistently between $60,000,000 and

$70,000,000. He would see that there was very little long-term debt, a book value of almost $7.00 per share, and a positive cash flow even during the period of earnings loss. At $10 a share, the company was being valued at little more than $20,000,000. The company had sales of $30 to $35 per common share, which was unusually high. Assuming that the management succeeded in establishing even a consistent 5% net profit on sales after taxes, the result would be earnings per share of $1.50 to $1.75. Even a conservative 15:1 price-earnings ratio in a growth industry like cosmetics would forecast a stock price rise at least to the mid $20's. Clearly, the constant speculative appeal of this stock would help support its market price and make it an attractive option-writing vehicle. Buyers of Calls, realizing the possibilities of a dramatic price rise, would be willing to pay attractive premiums for options.

On the basis of the above risk appraisal, the author accepted the six month and 10 day Straddle bid shown to him. The chance of a price decline seemed moderate at the strike price of $16, but would be quite low if the market price dropped to the low teens. Moreover, with a further decline in the market price, Helene Curtis could continue to be an attractive option-writing vehicle.

During the latter half of 1966 Helene Curtis stock continued to decline during a rather severe general market decline. However, it never went below the $10 to $12 floor. In early February, the Put portion of the Straddle was exercised with the market price of the stock at $12. Within days, a 95-day Straddle option bid was sold for a premium of $300. The percentile ranking curves confirmed it as an outstanding bid. The risk appraisal conducted several months ago was still considered valid although Helene Curtis reported further earnings losses. The author began purchasing stock and simultaneously selling Straddle options. There was no

Analysis of Actual Option Writing Transactions

lack of bids, offered through the option broker who was aware of the author's interest in the stock. In 1967, the author sold eleven Straddles at strike prices ranging from $12 to $14¾ and premiums in the range of $375 to $425. The gross income from the premiums amounted to $4,175. The net profit was slightly higher after deducting brokerage expenses and taking into account the profit on some lots of stock bought for less than the strike prices at which the options were sold. The Put portions of the Straddles were exercised four times; the Call portions exercised six times, and once neither portion of the Straddle was exercised, when the strike price and market price were identical at expiration. During the year, 300 to 500 shares costing $4,000 to $6,000 were held as security for the options. The percent return on investment was enhanced by the sale of an occasional naked option. At the end of the year, the market price of Helene Curtis was about $16, the same as the original strike price at which the first Straddle option was sold eighteen months earlier.

This is a striking example of the profits that an option writer can realize on a stock which would have been a disappointment to the conventional investor looking for price appreciation. The option buyers did not fare very well either. Assuming that each Straddle was converted to two Calls, the eleven options were the equivalent to twenty-two Calls sold. Of these, ten expired worthless since the author was put stock by the conversion house four times, and in one case neither component of the Straddle was exercised. Twelve of the Calls were probably exercised with only a partial recovery of the premium paid and certainly no significant profit on the investment in the premium by the option buyer. Currently (June, 1968) Helene Curtis stock is selling in the low $20s because of recent earnings improvement and the firm prospect of future earnings gains. The author still has several Straddles outstanding at strike prices in the $14 to $15 range. The Call portions of these Straddles will in all likelihood be exercised with handsome profits for the option buyers.

Here is an example in which the option buyers profited more than the option writer: In September, 1967, the author was shown a six month and 10 day Straddle bid for a premium of $325 on American Photocopy, an office-copying equipment company, at a strike price of $9½. The graphs showed an over 90% return on investment with simultaneous purchase of the stock at the $9½ market price. The percentile ranking curves confirmed that this bid was well up in the upper quarter. Obviously some option buyer was extremely enthusiastic about the prospects for this stock, assuming, as was likely, that he was purchasing Calls after conversion. Risk appraisal revealed an interesting situation. In 1966, American Photocopy had shown consistent quarterly earnings losses, the culmination of a steady downtrend in earnings and a subsequent decline in market price to a low of $6. In the first two quarters of 1967, small profits led to a rise in market price to $9 to $10 which had been maintained for a few months. The option broker revealed the generally-known fact that the company's promising new office copying machine was beginning to sell very well. It was reasonable to conclude that the potential earnings per share would improve. The risk of a market price decline did not appear substantial at the $9½ strike price of the option. Moreover, glamorous office copying equipment stocks could be expected to attract speculators, at least at the then current market price levels.

The company was financially healthy with negligible long-term debt, and no preferred stock, but with eight million shares of common stock outstanding. Sales in the near-term future were expected to be $40,000,000 to $50,000,000 or

$5 to $6 per share. Even if profits improved substantially the large number of shares outstanding would prevent spectacular gains in earnings per share. To justify a substantial price increase in the stock, the investment community would have to foresee a high price-earnings ratio in the near-term future. Such an evaluation, however, seemed likely because this was a glamor stock. On the other hand, if earnings growth faltered, or there were losses, the market price might fall dramatically if the price level was substantially higher than the $9½ strike price. There appeared to be substantial risk in writing options on American Photocopy at prices much higher than the $9½ bid being considered.

The author accepted the six month and 10 day Straddle offered for $325, and purchased stock as security at the $9½ strike price. Within three months he sold three more six month and 10 day Straddles, the first at a strike price of $10 and two more at a strike price of $12. All options were sold with the simultaneous purchase of stock as security. The situation turned out not to be very attractive for the sale of naked options. In December 1966, just after the sale of the last two Straddles, American Photocopy climbed from $12 to $22 in little over one month before settling back to the high teens. With the stock price above $20, the Call portions of the two Straddles written four months previously were exercised. At strike prices of $9½ and $10, the option buyers did splendidly. They probably invested $200 to $225 as the premium for their Calls for a net profit of $800 to $900 each. The author, as option writer, did not begrudge them their spectacular profits. His percent return on investment of approximately 150% from the first two Calls suited him very well.

The early exercise of the first two Calls would have given the option writer short-term profits equivalent to the premiums less brokerage expenses if he had delivered the stock originally purchased as security for the first two Straddles sold. However, the option broker was directed to deliver the 200 shares purchased at $12 as security for the two latest Straddle options sold. Instead of short-term profits, small short-term losses were realized and the stock purchased originally at $9½ and $10 became the security for the two options written at the strike price of $12. If, as was likely, the Call portions of these two Straddles were exercised more than six months after purchase of the stock at $9½ and $10, the option writer would realize an additional $450 long-term gain.

Laboratory for Electronics (LFE) is a relatively small electronic equipment manufacturer listed on the N. Y. Stock Exchange. The stock has been a favorite with the author for the past four years and is one of those for which he has developed a "feel." He has bought and sold approximately 2,000 shares for a profit of several thousand dollars. Some, but not all, of the transactions have been option sales. The rest have been the purchases of a conventional investor —speculating on price rises which in some cases brought a greater return on investment than an option sale. In other cases the author bought stock and waited until it appreciated substantially before selling options on it. His profit in these cases was the premium plus the difference between his purchase price and the strike price.

The author has found LFE an attractive speculative vehicle because of the extremely "thin" market of 1.3 million shares outstanding, and its consequent great volatility. During the past few years company sales have remained in the $40,000,000 to $60,000,000 range, although earnings have been erratic. During this period, however, the management has shifted over from an almost exclusive dependence on military contracts to a much broader line of attractive commercial products. The author first began purchasing LFE stock for speculation in 1964 at $7 per share after the stock had declined precipitously from a 1961 high of around $60. The company was losing money because of the drop in sales resulting from completion of large military contracts. The management recognized the problem and was already diversifying to include potentially very significant commercial products. The company was financially sound, although, incredibly, the investment community valued the whole company including its patents, and hundreds of highly trained professional employees at only $8,000,000 to $9,-000,000. The book value of buildings, equipment, land, etc. alone was considerably more.

The author purchased 100 shares of LFE stock in March, 1966, at $12⅝. Anticipating a rapid price rise, he was reluctant to sell Calls and Straddles using this stock as security. A Put, however, was a different matter. In October, 1966, he accepted an opportunity to sell a six month and 10 day Put at $15⅝ for a premium of $225. He expected the Put to expire unexercised as the stock rose in price. In less than two months the stock advanced another four points and this time he sold a six month and 10 day Call at $19¾ for a premium of $312.50. Opportunities to sell Straddles were also available but the Call was considered a more cautious investment. The percent return on investment for this Call was 42%, which put it well up in the top percentile quarter for a Call. Option buyers, seeing the potential of the stock, were willing to pay very attractive premiums. Both the Put and Call options eventually expired unexercised, with the premium income counting as ordinary income and reported under "other income" on the tax return. When the Call expired in June, 1967, a six month and 10 day Straddle was sold at a strike price of $18⅝ for a premium of $500. The Call portion of the Straddle was exercised in December with the stock at $26⅛, near its high for the year. If the author had delivered the stock that he had bought at $12⅝ as security for the Straddle, he would have realized a long-term gain of $900. When the Put portion of the Straddle expired unexercised, he would have been taxed on the $225 premium as a short-term gain. Rather than pay these taxes the author bought stock in the market at $26⅛ and delivered it to the option buyer for a short-term loss of $475. This loss was applied against the substantial short-term gains resulting from the expired and unexercised components of Straddles sold during the year.

The stock purchased originally at $12⅝ was now available for further option sales. The 30-day rule prohibited outright sale of the stock for that length of time, and with its very substantial rise the stock appeared vulnerable to at least a temporary price decline. The author called his option broker to see if he could sell a Call, but definitely not a Straddle with the risk of being put the stock at what the author considered a dangerously high price. A potential buyer offered a premium of $225 for a 95-day Call, but the author insisted on $250. Compromising, the buyer paid $250 but the strike price was reduced from $26⅛ to $25⅞. In March, 1968, the Call expired unexercised with the stock price declining to $20 per share. Had a Straddle been sold instead of a Call the stock would have been put at $25⅞ when its market value was only $20.

While the author regards himself as a competent, experienced option writer, his transactions have not been a series of uninterrupted successes. Here is one which turned out rather poorly.

The author has been involved in many profitable transactions with Lehigh Valley Industries, listed on the N. Y. Stock Exchange. In July, 1967, he sold two six month and 10 day Straddles on the stock at a strike price of $9¼ for $250 each with simultaneous purchase of stock as security.

Analysis of Actual Option Writing Transactions

The bid was not outstandingly attractive, for the percentile ranking curve showed the percent return on investment near the 50 percentile curve. However, he felt the risk was low. For the next few months the stock hovered around $8. In December, with only a little more than a month to go before the expiration of the Straddles, the author sold the 200 shares of stock held as security for $9. He wanted the cash to take advantage of a fine option-writing opportunity and he thought there was little risk in leaving the Straddles naked for so short a time. He felt it probable that the Puts would be exercised and the Calls would expire. Even if the Calls were exercised, the author could still make a profit if he were forced to buy stock in the market at a 1 or 1½ point markup. That was the maximum rise he predicted for this dormant stock. He was wrong. Within a matter of days the stock advanced to a high of $13¾. The Calls were exercised in mid-January, 1968, with the stock at $12¾ at which price 200 shares were purchased and delivered to the option buyer. Instead of the $450 net profit the author would have realized if he had held on to his stock security, he sustained a $300 net loss.

The author has engaged in other naked transactions which have turned out quite profitably. It is apparent, however, that selling naked options is risky and option writers will inevitably lose on some of them. From another standpoint the example above bears a message to all option writers including those who would never sell naked options. Once in a while the option writer will engage in a transaction on a familiar stock for which he has a real "feel" yet everything that could possibly go wrong will go wrong. These unfortunate situations should be taken in stride, the transactions studied to profit from any mistakes, and the next bid weighed a little more closely.